COASTAL GARDERN DESIGN by Mark Whyte

© Copyright Mark Whyte, 2024

Mark Whyte has asserted his right to be identified as the author of this work in accordance with sections 77 and 78 of the Copyright, Designs and Patents Act 1988.

Content editorial : Emma Whyte

While the author has used their best efforts in preparing this book, they make no representations or warranties with respect to the accuracy or completeness of the contents of this book and specifically disclaim any implied warranties of merchantability or fitness for a particular purpose.

No warranty may be created or extended by sales representatives or written sales materials. The advice and strategies contained herein may not be suitable for your situation. You should consult with a professional when appropriate.

Neither the publisher nor the author shall be liable for any loss of profit or any other commercial or domestic damages, including but not limited to special, incidental, consequential, personal, or other damages.

All rights reserved. No part of this book may be reproduced or distributed in any form without prior written permission from the author, with the exception of non-commercial uses permitted by copyright law.

No part of this book may be reproduced or transmitted by any means, except as permitted by UK copyright law or the author. For licensing requests, please contact the author at hello@ivyandwhyte.com.

For permission to publish, distribute or otherwise reproduce this work, please contact the author at hello@ivyandwhyte.com

CONTENTS

01 Living By The Sea
Page 14-25

02 Flora and Fauna
Page 26-33

03 Coastal Climate
Page 34-43

04 UK Coastal Gardens
Page 44-79

05 Ivy & Whyte Example
Page 80-87

06 Materials and Features
Page 92-121

07 Colour
Page 122-136

08 Texture, Shape and Form
Page 136-155

09 Design Preparation
Page 156-165

10 Measure and Draw
Page 166-181

11 Plants and Planting
Page 182-217

12 Environmental
Page 218-223

FOREWORD

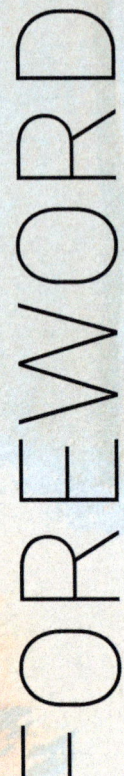

Having grown up in a Kentish coastal town, I've been immersed in its exhilarating energy all my life. I spent most of my formative years chasing storms and exploring pebbly beaches. I often stood on the promenade, risking my life to experience the energy of a 60mph gale! As an adult, I've relished blustery dog walks, sea swimming and coastal photography and am constantly inspired by its ever-changing moods.

In 2014, after a long career in gardening and landscaping, I found myself on the garden design path and created Ivy & Whyte Garden Design. Over the years, our designs have evolved naturally into themes inspired by the coastal landscape and we've recently expanded to be able to offer Ivy and Whyte Sussex as well as Ivy and Whyte Kent, covering pretty much the whole of the South East coast.

Coastal Garden Design requires special attention where plant and material choices are concerned and we are passionate about ensuring our designs are modern, thoughtful and timeless. We have had great fun and excitement working with our clients over the years on some amazing coastal concepts, which very often contain a range of bespoke ideas, such as sea groyne water features and unique metal sculptures.

In 2016 we challenged ourselves to create a coastal-themed show garden for the world's largest flower show at Hampton Court. The garden incorporated a giant 3m high and 14m long cresting wave made from 800 lengths of steam bent wood. This huge sculpture was surrounded by a natural coastal landscape inspired by Dungeness in Kent. It had a fantastic reception at the show and gained us a Silver Guilt RHS medal. After a year spent on designing, building and even growing the garden (we grew most of our plants from seed), we were certainly tired, but exhilarated by the end of the project.

We hope you enjoy this book and that it gives you the motivation to get stuck into creating your own coastal space. Filled with inspirational ideas, we think it's the best place to start.

We hold regular Coastal Design workshops in the South East of England. If you want to find out more, you can register at **www.ivyandwhyte.com.**

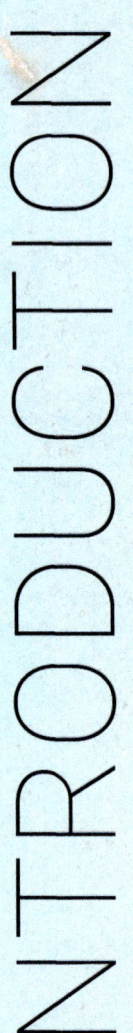

INTRODUCTION

Despite being such a small group of islands, the UK coastline is nearly 18,000km long (Ordnance Survey) and is home to approximately 5.3 million residents. However, regardless of where you might find yourself within UK borders, you're never more than a 2 hour drive away.

This book has been designed to take you on a journey, beginning with a trip through seaside living - what it means to live coastally, how it impacts people and wildlife and how to get the most out of living by the sea.

We visited some beautiful gardens around the coast of England and Scotland, all with their individual challenges and styles. We chatted to the people who know them inside out - the designers and those that live within them - to really explore what it means to create a coastal garden.

In our final section we'll talk you through how to design your own coastal garden, the materials and plants to consider, colour, shape and form and the specifics of basic design, so that you can use the inspiration gained to design your very own coastal garden.

It has very often been said that living near the sea can significantly improve your mental health. The colours associated with coastal areas, such as fresh blue, serene cream and deep brown hues, evoke feelings of calm and peace and the myriad of textures, sounds and smells to be found around the coastline are a feast for the senses.

Imagine bringing that feeling to your garden - if you live beside the sea, a cleverly designed coastal garden can bring more of the sea to you and add a vast sense of extra space. If you live in the middle of the city, you can design a garden that takes you away from the hustle and bustle for a while and enjoy your very own piece of coastal paradise.

01

A deep breath of salty sea air can invigorate you and the sound of waves crashing with steadfast regularity can give a feeling of primitive comfort whether you've got fond memories of the coast or even if you've never even been before.

The UK coastline is varied - rugged stone, soft sand, rough grass, stunning sand dunes, pristine chalk cliffs - all unique habitats that provide food and shelter for birds, insects, reptiles and sea creatures of all shapes and sizes. The coastline is strong and steady, but ever-changing.

Many coastal dwellers would agree that spending time by the coast can give you a sense of renewed energy and vigour and I know many people who believe that it benefits their health and wellbeing.

The main reasons for this are likely to be an increase in physical activity, a natural stress reduction and a higher likelihood of positive social interactions, along with a tendency to better air quality - coastal air generally carries more oxygen and minerals than inland air.

COMMUNITY

Community is a key part of happy living and very often a natural part of coastal living. Most coastal towns are fairly small communities, and being a part of a small community can often mean a high likelihood of regular social interaction and a joining together of like-minded people.

Being part of a community gives a sense of belonging and purpose, which in turn helps to support mental health. There are many opportunities to spend time taking part in hobbies and other activities whilst breathing in the fresh sea air and these experiences can be very beneficial to our physical health.

A stretch of sand or pebbles along the beach is a magnet for dog walkers and the perfect place for dogs and owners alike to meet new friends.

A vibrant coastal town attracts an array of visitors, and this increases the chance of meeting new people and expanding the community experience.

The coast attracts people with a similar desire to find peace and joy from the seaside, and many who, as a result, consciously choose to make it their home. Very often, we hold happy memories of holidays to the beach as children and this can evoke many positive emotions and feelings of comfort and wellbeing.

PHYSICAL HEALTH

We all know that keeping fit is vital to ensure we can enjoy life to the fullest. We're all aware that when exposed to nature, our muscle tension, anxiety, blood pressure, heart rate and stress hormone levels all decrease, so taking part in regular outdoor activities can be incredibly beneficial to our physical health.

Regular active hobbies such as swimming and walking can improve chronic conditions such as dementia and cardiovascular disease, and although too much sun can be a bad thing, just the right amount increases our vitamin D levels, which in turn helps our bones to stay strong and healthy.

There are so many opportunities for getting involved in healthy activities within your local community along the coast. With easy access to the beach, kayaking, sailing, sea swimming and surfing are just some of the ways you can benefit your physical health.

Sea swimming has seen a huge surge in popularity in recent years and it's no wonder - immersing yourself in salt water helps to heal your body - it's rich in magnesium, chloride, sodium, potassium, iodine and sulphur, which all have anti-inflammatory effects on the skin. Cold water swimming boosts your immune system, gives you a natural high, burns calories and reduces stress.

Whether you prefer to have a leisurely swim, a relaxing walk or take part in a water sport, such as kayaking or kite-surfing, the physical benefits of exercising by the coast can be varied and vast.

MENTAL HEALTH

Being in nature, or even just looking at images of it, has been proven to reduce anger, stress and fear and increase feelings of happiness and contentment. It's believed that simply looking out to sea, along with other areas of open water, promotes a chemical called dopamine, which is connected to happiness and developing a more positive thought process.

The mental health benefits of living by the coast link beautifully with the physical benefits discussed before. A good level of social interaction and physical sport helps to support your mental health. Studies have also shown that people tend to experience better quality sleep if they are by the coast and we all know the bountiful benefits of a good night's sleep.

With its natural dopamine and serotonin releases, coastal life does wonders for your mental health. Activities such as walking, running, yoga classes and meditation are fantastic ways to support your physical and mental wellbeing.

There is nothing quite like meditating on the beach, surrounded by the energy of the waves and their regular hypnotic sound, then opening your eyes to drink in the mesmerising view of a beautiful deep pink, red and purple sunrise.

02

There are over 1200 different species of plants and animals that have made the UK coast their home. One thing is for sure, they have all adapted well to harsh conditions and thrive in places that other UK species would not.

Coastal plants are generally very tough and have adapted to survive in some mighty challenging conditions. Exposed to salty winds, sea-spray and little rainfall, these plants are quite happy living in sand or shingle - their roots strong enough to withstand being beaten about by the wind.

The mammals, birds and insects along the coastline have got to be equally as resilient. From beautiful sea anemone in rockpools, graceful jellyfish and colourful algae to bossy seagulls, incredible whales and playful dolphins, the coast is bustling with life.

In this chapter, we'll talk you through a small number of the different species that make up the UK coastal ecosystem. Overall, the UK coastline provides a habitat for a rich and diverse array of wildlife, making it an extremely important area for conservation and preservation.

The structurally beautiful sea holly (*Eryngium maritimum*) is possibly the first plant that comes to mind when we think of coastal plants. With gorgeous blue globe-like flowers on misty-blue spiky foliage, it's a stunner year-round.

Happy pretty much anywhere, the red valerian (*Centranthus ruber*) brings a touch of the wild. It loves to grow in free-draining soil and can often be seen growing with wild abandon on old walls and rocky cliffs. A long flowering perennial with nectar-rich flowers.

The tall blue spikes of viper's-bugloss (*Echium vulgare*) can be found on chalk grassland, sand dunes and cliffs. Its funnel-shaped flowers provide food for many insects including bees and butterflies from May through to September.

Yellow-horned poppy (*Glaucium flavum*) is a beautiful annual, which is said to have the largest seed pods of any British plant. Green horn-like seed pods of up to 30cm long produce copious amounts of seed after flowering.

Sea campion (*Silene maritima*) is a dainty white flower related to the carnation. It loves a rugged clifftop and folklore suggests it should never be picked because it tempts death!

Straight and prim, the globular pink flowers of sea thrift (*Armeria maritima*) can be spotted in wild, coastal areas of the UK and are at their best sprawling across the top of rocky cliffs.

Sea kale (*Crambe maritima*) is a native that is right at home on the windy shores of England, Wales and Scotland. It has tough, waxy leaves and honey-scented clusters of white flowers which appear in summer.

The young umbrella-shaped flowers of the wild carrot (*Daucus carota*) change from a reddish hue through to white and although its leaves and roots do indeed smell of carrots, the roots are very different to the carrot you'd find on a dinner table.

A full-sun lover like most coastal plants, the common mallow (*Malva sylvestris*) has beautiful funnel-shaped mauve flowers striped with purple. Providing nectar all summer long, its flowers are a favourite for many insects.

The common gorse (*Ulex europaeus*) thrives on heaths and coastal grasslands and can be seen for miles around - a large shrub with coconut-scented yellow flowers, it's needle-like leaves protect birds and therefore make it an ideal nest site for lots of species, providing food for them too.

The teasel (*Dipsacus fullonum*) is tall and spiky and provides a fantastic food source for wildlife, with rings of purple flowers for insects during the summer months, followed by spiky brown seed heads which provide food for birds during the autumn and winter.

Growing happily in poor, well-drained soil, the California poppy (*Eschscholzia californica*) needs full sun for its stunning yellow-orange flowers to open and although they may be lacking in nectar, they are a good pollen source and a favourite of bees.

Dolphins and porpoises are often seen along the UK coastline, particularly in areas with a strong tidal flow, one of the most familiar species being the delightful bottlenose dolphin.

Humpback and minke whales can occasionally be spotted from the coast and grey or common seals, known for their distinctive vocalisations and playful behaviour, can be seen basking on rocks or swimming in the water.

At low tide in the UK, many coastal areas become adventure playgrounds for young and old alike, as vibrant life is much more accessible thanks to the emerging rockpools. From crabs lurking under rocks to fragile starfish or the beautiful tentacles of a sea anemone, there is so much to find.

The UK coastline is famous for its fantastic variety of native and visiting birds including gulls, puffins and cormorants.

Common seals, known for their distinctive vocalisations and playful behaviour, can be seen basking on rocks or swimming.

From the delightful little sanderling, often seen running back and forth at great speed up and down the shingle, to the much larger and robust Herring Gull, we are not only lucky to have a large number of native birds who make their homes around our coastline year-round, but we are treated annually to an influx of overseas visitors too.

Of all the UK's coastal birds, one of our most favourite must be the Common Puffin, with its distinctive black and white plumage and brightly coloured beak. The UK is home to over one million puffins spread from the west coast to the east.

The UK coastline is also home to a diverse range of insects, including butterflies, bees, and dragonflies. These insects are important pollinators and play a crucial role in maintaining the balance of the coastal ecosystem.

The United Kingdom is home to over one million puffins spread from the west coast to the east.

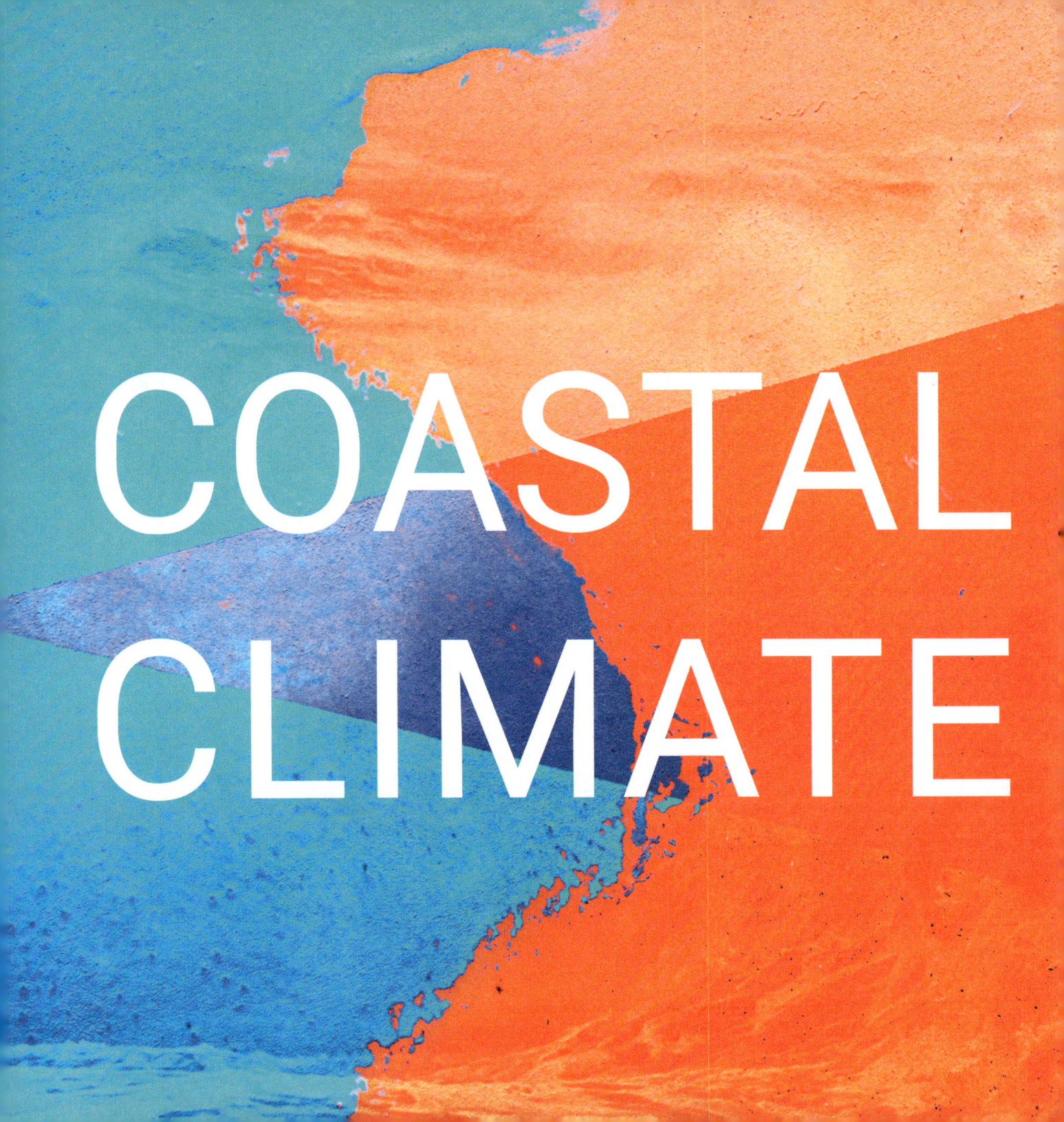

03

The United Kingdom is surrounded by water and its coastline is the longest in Europe. Living in a temperate climate and thanks to the Gulf Stream, we generally avoid extreme cold winters and harsh drought conditions. Our winds are principally from the west to south-west, but every direction brings challenges with it for people residing on the coast.

There are many different micro-climates along the UK coast which often makes general weather forecasts redundant thanks to very localised patterns. It is worth thinking about this if you plan to build a new garden on the coast. The coast can provide us with some of our weather extremes - from high winds to heavy rainfall, it can be a dramatic place to live.

One thing is certain - our climate is warming up along with the rest of the world. By how much we cannot be sure, but whatever the impact, it will be felt around the coastline. Plants we would never have expected to grow could thrive in future years and current favourites could become legends of the past.

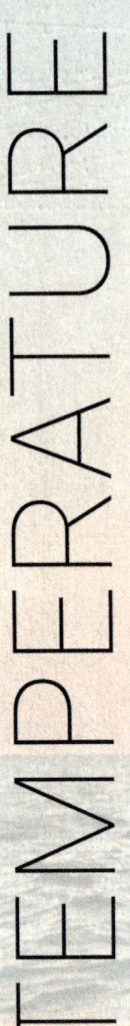

TEMPERATURE

Our temperate climate has distinct seasonal changes, although a snow day is more of a rare occurrence in the south. In fact, in southern areas, lawnmowers can now be heard well into late autumn and early winter.

The coastline of the UK has many micro-climates. One of the most noticeable is in Cornwall which has an average yearly temperature of around 11 ° c. In direct line of the Atlantic and the jet stream, this area keeps a steady temperature and suffers very few frosts. The result is that plants which would be impossible to grow in other parts of the UK can grow quite happily here. Coastal gardens in Cornwall can become near-tropical paradises.

> We are an island producing the most amazing range of plant life around the coasts. Temperature plays a vital role in their development and flowering times.

On the other hand, the east of the country can very often be battered by the 'beast from the east' winter storms. One week of a north easterly wind direction in a polar winter is enough to send many tender plants to their end. This is true of the whole east coast from Scotland down to Kent.

In 2022, the UK recorded over 40 ° c for the first time, breaking records and it seems that this may become more of a regular occurrence because of climate change. Drought is becoming the new normal and we naturally expect a greater number of hosepipe bans in the future and a lot more focus on saving water.

We are an island producing the most amazing range of plants around our coasts, temperature plays a vital role in their development and flowering times. Coastal areas of the UK always struggle to become winter wonderlands and if you are close to the coast and at sea level, a bit of sleet is very often all that can be expected in the winter months.

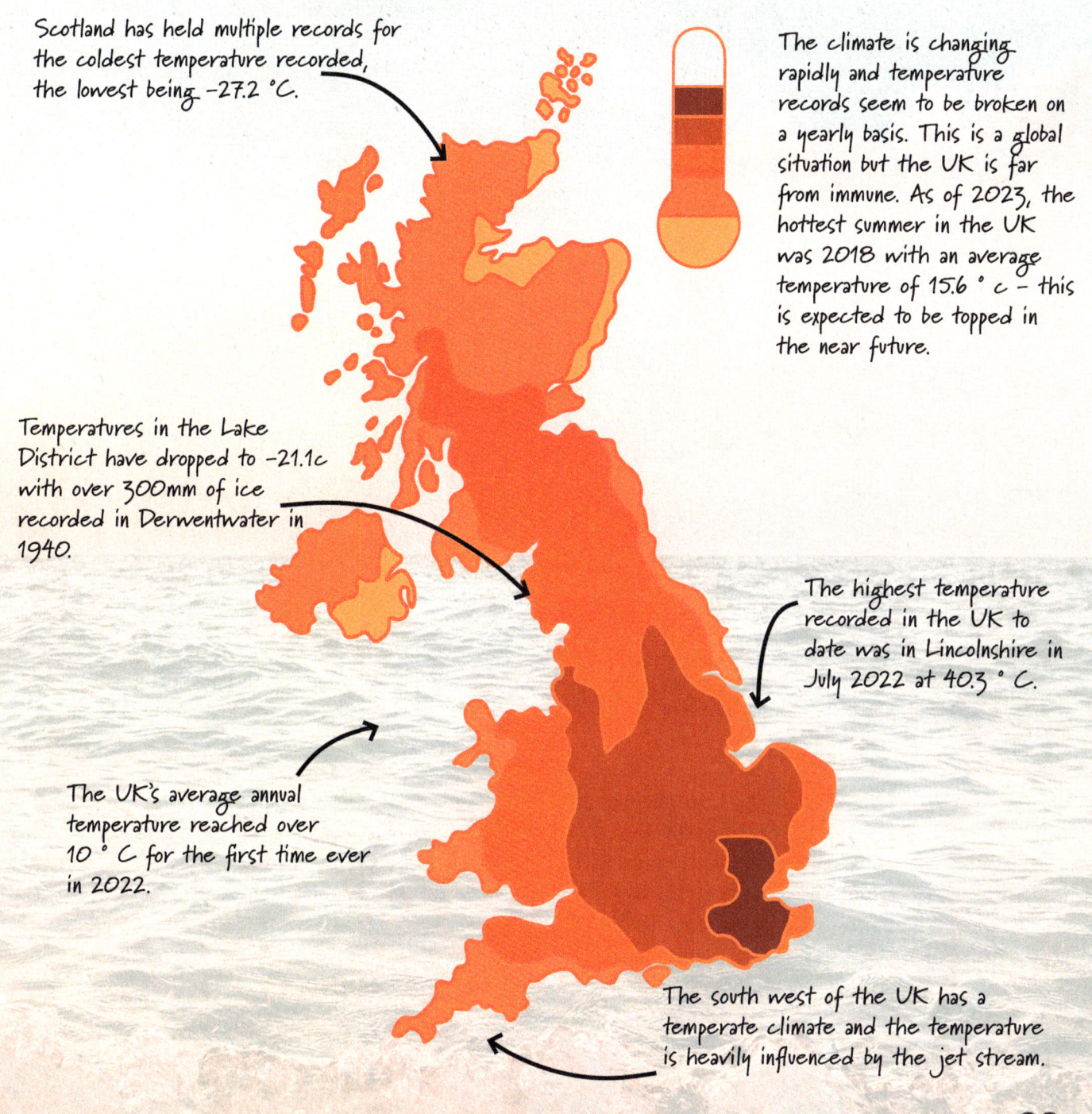

Scotland has held multiple records for the coldest temperature recorded, the lowest being -27.2 °C.

The climate is changing rapidly and temperature records seem to be broken on a yearly basis. This is a global situation but the UK is far from immune. As of 2023, the hottest summer in the UK was 2018 with an average temperature of 15.6 °c – this is expected to be topped in the near future.

Temperatures in the Lake District have dropped to -21.1c with over 300mm of ice recorded in Derwentwater in 1940.

The highest temperature recorded in the UK to date was in Lincolnshire in July 2022 at 40.3 °C.

The UK's average annual temperature reached over 10 °C for the first time ever in 2022.

The south west of the UK has a temperate climate and the temperature is heavily influenced by the jet stream.

33

RAINFALL

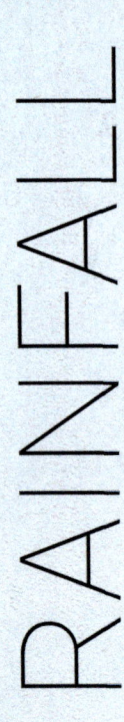

Rainfall levels in the UK are varied and heavily controlled by the jet stream. Low pressure systems formed in the Atlantic are driven across to our shores by the jet stream and much of the rainfall is dropped on the western areas of the UK with the coastline taking the first offerings.

Typical frontal bands of precipitation that are associated with the low pressures do fragment as they move across the country and can end up giving a few splashes of rain or just cloud to the east. From west to east the average yearly rainfall varies from around 600mm to 1000mm.

The driest area is East Anglia, which is hardly surprising considering it's tucked out the way of westerly winds. This has a big effect on planting, and as mentioned before, low rainfall can cause problems for plant growth in the South and East regions.

Designing your garden to capture and manage rainfall can support a diverse range of wildlife.

Rain can add a magical touch to your garden design - glistening raindrops on petals and leaves or the soothing sound of rain falling on different surfaces. It can enhance the visual and auditory experience of your outdoor space.

Rainfall contributes to the creation of microhabitats within your garden. Puddles can become miniature ecosystems for insects, birds, and amphibians. Designing your garden to capture and manage rainfall can support a diverse range of wildlife. Rainwater harvesting is becoming more popular and is a fantastic way to ensure that we don't waste this precious resource. In the not-too-distant future it may become essential.

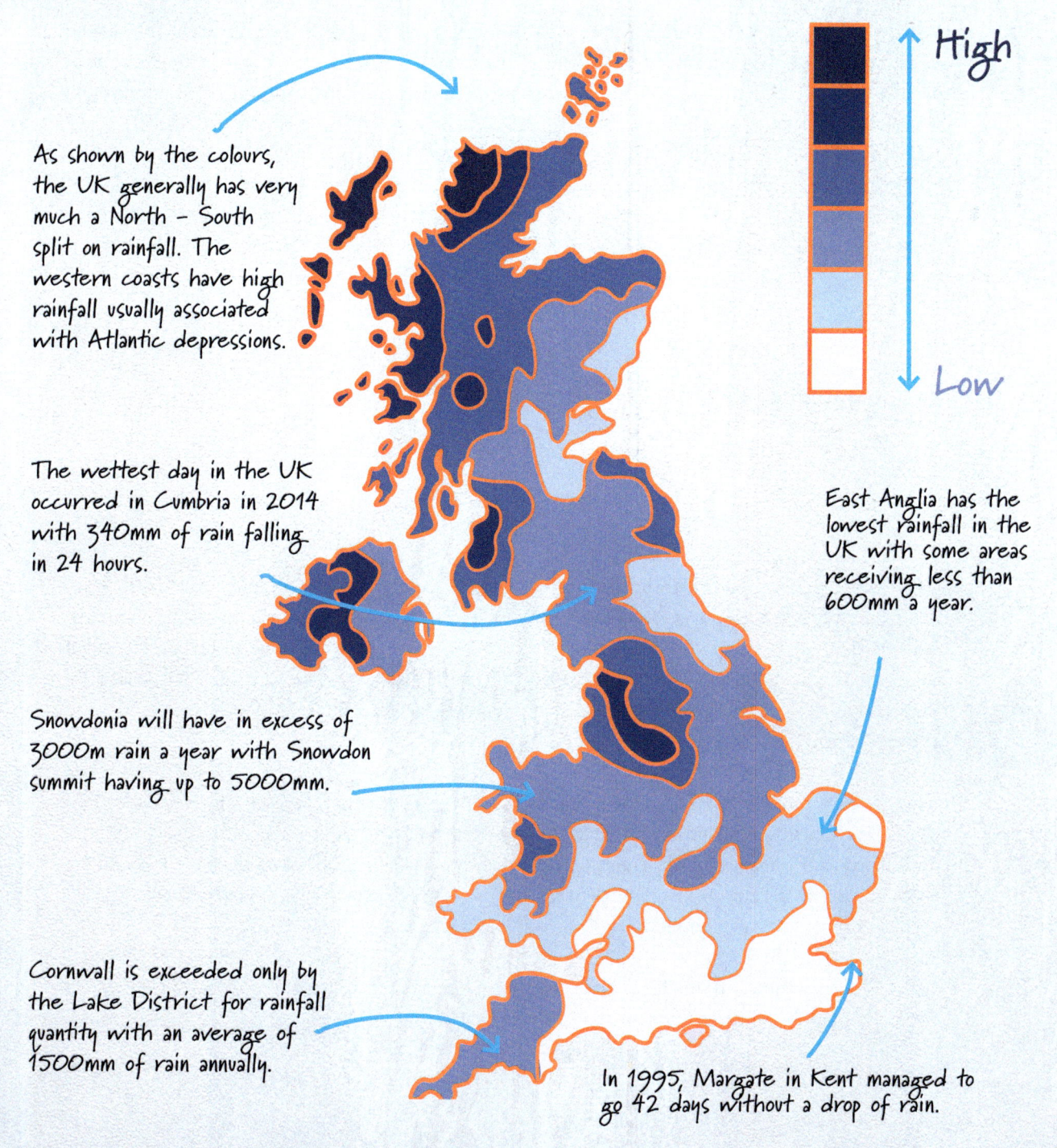

As shown by the colours, the UK generally has very much a North – South split on rainfall. The western coasts have high rainfall usually associated with Atlantic depressions.

The wettest day in the UK occurred in Cumbria in 2014 with 340mm of rain falling in 24 hours.

Snowdonia will have in excess of 3000m rain a year with Snowdon summit having up to 5000mm.

Cornwall is exceeded only by the Lake District for rainfall quantity with an average of 1500mm of rain annually.

High

Low

East Anglia has the lowest rainfall in the UK with some areas receiving less than 600mm a year.

In 1995, Margate in Kent managed to go 42 days without a drop of rain.

35

WIND

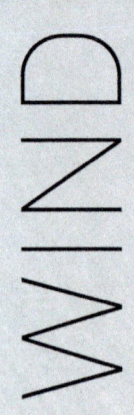

We are a windy island with the Atlantic Ocean to the west, the cooler North Sea to the east and north and the English Channel to the South. Low pressure systems track across the Atlantic and usually make landfall mid-country, delivering strong winds and rain. Our strongest winds come from this direction.

Each wind direction brings with it different conditions which are best shown on the map opposite. Naturally, on the coast we can expect to see the strongest winds. The west and south coasts are regularly battered with autumnal storms as is the North of Scotland and islands.

The Rustling of leaves and the gentle breeze of the wind moving through coastal vegetation contribute to the overall sensory experience of your garden

Wind will bring salt with it and during strong winds, this can be carried fairly far inland, which can have a big effect on our garden plants. If you are by the coast and thinking about changing your garden, it's worth researching taller plants to make sure they are structurally sound and able to deal with salt-laden air. Another consideration with gardens and wind is the boundaries of your property. Fencing should be checked and looked after. A rickety old fence is no match for a force 10 storm.

The coastal wind brings an ever-changing atmosphere to your garden. You can celebrate this dynamic quality by choosing plants with foliage that dances in the breeze - adding movement and life to your outdoor space. The rustling of leaves and the gentle breeze of the wind moving through coastal vegetation contribute to the overall sensory experience of your garden. The sound of the wind can also act as a calming soundtrack.

Of course, we can spend much of the year under higher pressure with light winds. This warms up the land and can make our coast feel almost tropical.

ARCTIC

Bringing wet weather and cold, snowy winters, the northerly wind is much spoken about but doesn't occur very often and although showery for the North, the South will be drier.

POLAR CONTINENTAL

Bringing dry summers but snowy winters. Usually associated with high pressure this direction offers fairly settled conditions but can be brutally cold in winter.

POLAR MARITIME

Bringing wet and cold showery conditions. These are felt most notably in northern areas, with southern counties fairing better.

TROPICAL CONTINENTAL

Hottest air mass in UK bringing hot, dry summers. Also this direction can bring cold continental winter weather and thunderstorms.

TROPICAL MARITIME

Cloudy and mild weather but often quite wet. Our prevailing wind direction, which is associated with the jet stream and Atlantic low pressure systems.

37

SOIL TYPE

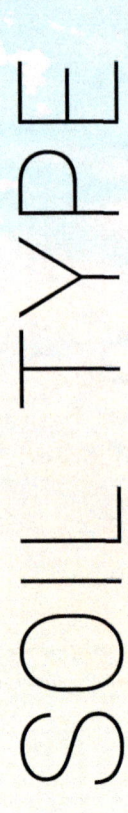

Every plant has its optimum soil type as all are adapted to their own special conditions. Where one plant will thrive, another will perish. Plants do survive in soil that is not ideal, but it doesn't guarantee the best result.

The pH level of soil is important as it determines what nutrients are available to plants. Nitrogen, phosphorus and potassium are key nutrients for any plant, needed in various quantities depending on the species. There are ways to adjust the pH level of soil by adding wood ashes or organic matter, depending on whether the soil is too acidic or alkaline.

The easiest way to test levels is to equally measure a sample of soil and distilled water, agitate and leave the mixture for half an hour before draining the water into a glass. Use a pH test strip to indicate the soil nutrient structure.

> There are a number of ways to adjust the pH level of soil by adding a variety of mediums depending on whether the soil is too acidic or alkaline.

Soil drainage is another factor that has a key impact on the growth of plants. Different types of soil have different levels of drainage. Soil examples include loam, sand, chalk, peat and clay.

In the south and east of England, coastal soil tends to be quite chalky or heavy clay. On the West Coast, it's more likely to be a more loamy soil and Northern England and Scotland tend to be more peaty and sandy.

The map on this page gives a very broad idea of soil types in the UK. Local variations will occur. Always check your soil type before planting.

- 🟠 Igneous and metamorphic
- 🟣 Limestones and sandstones
- 🔵 Limestones and shale
- 🟢 Sandstones
- 🟠 Limestone and clay
- 🟣 Chalk
- 🟢 Sands, clay, chalk

Soils in Scotland tend to be acidic and carbon-rich but relatively low in nutrients.

Limestone soil is generally alkaline but good for planting. This can be found with shale.

Chalky soils are generally low in nutrients due to the fast drainage. They are alkaline which is worth bearing in mind with plants that prefer acid-rich soil.

Clay soil is high in nutrients and when broken up can be very good for your plants.

39

COASTAL

GARDENS

UK COASTAL GARDENS

04

The previous few pages have hopefully given you some idea of the diversity of the UK climate. Although the UK has a general temperate climate, we also have many micro-climates which can affect how to plan a successful coastal garden.

We've chosen four very different locations to provide examples which highlight the differences and challenges that can come with developing your very own coastal space.

The following pages will introduce you to some beautiful and successful gardens from around our coastline. Each garden has played well to its own special circumstances - due to the different climate challenges each area faces, the difference in soil type and the preferences of each of the designers and their clients, these examples show you the many different approaches that can be explored when designing your own garden and ensuring it works for you.

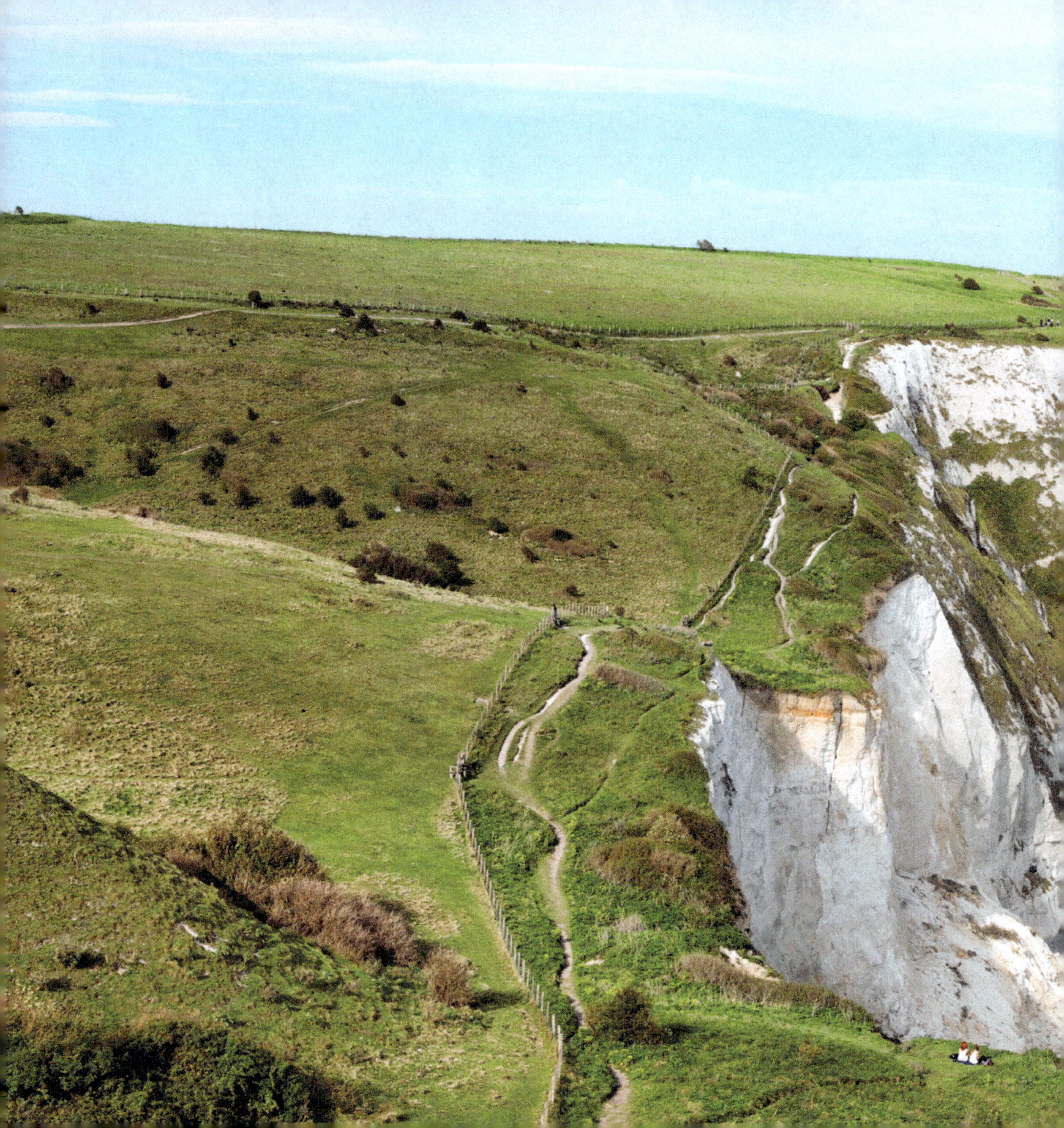

John Humphreys
johnhumphreyssculpture.com

SOUTH EAST

Garden Location..

The garden is located in stunning Normans Bay in East Sussex and lies directly on the beach. This brings some very demanding challenges, but equally enables the garden to have amazing character and diversity. One of the most enjoyable aspects of this garden is the shelter given by the house from front to back.
On the sea side, garden planting is successfully limited to the core plants that thrive naturally on a shingle beach.

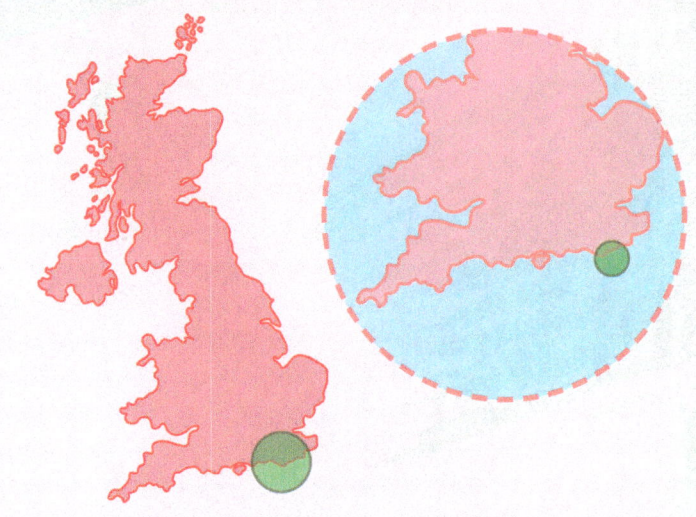

URANIUM GLASS

In John's front garden, a 5 metre sea groyne stands upright with pieces of coloured glass nestled within natural crevices along its length, each playfully reflecting and change in the light. It is beautiful to watch and is in no way intrusive to the natural environment around it.

47

'I allow the garden to have control... I work with it, creating a wonderful nature design balance'

There is very little soil on the beach side and the plants in this area need to be able to grow in the shingle and obviously take the brunt of the channel storms.

The back garden is much more sheltered than the front, which has given John the opportunity to include a larger range of plant species. The different climate, just 10 metres or so away, has given him the chance to grow many plants which would not tolerate the harsh conditions in the front.

The garden is adorned with favourites such as *Centranthus* and *Erigeron* 'sea breeze'. Dotted amongst the other plants, *crambe maritima* grows where it likes and John is very keen to go along with this - happy to be directed by nature.

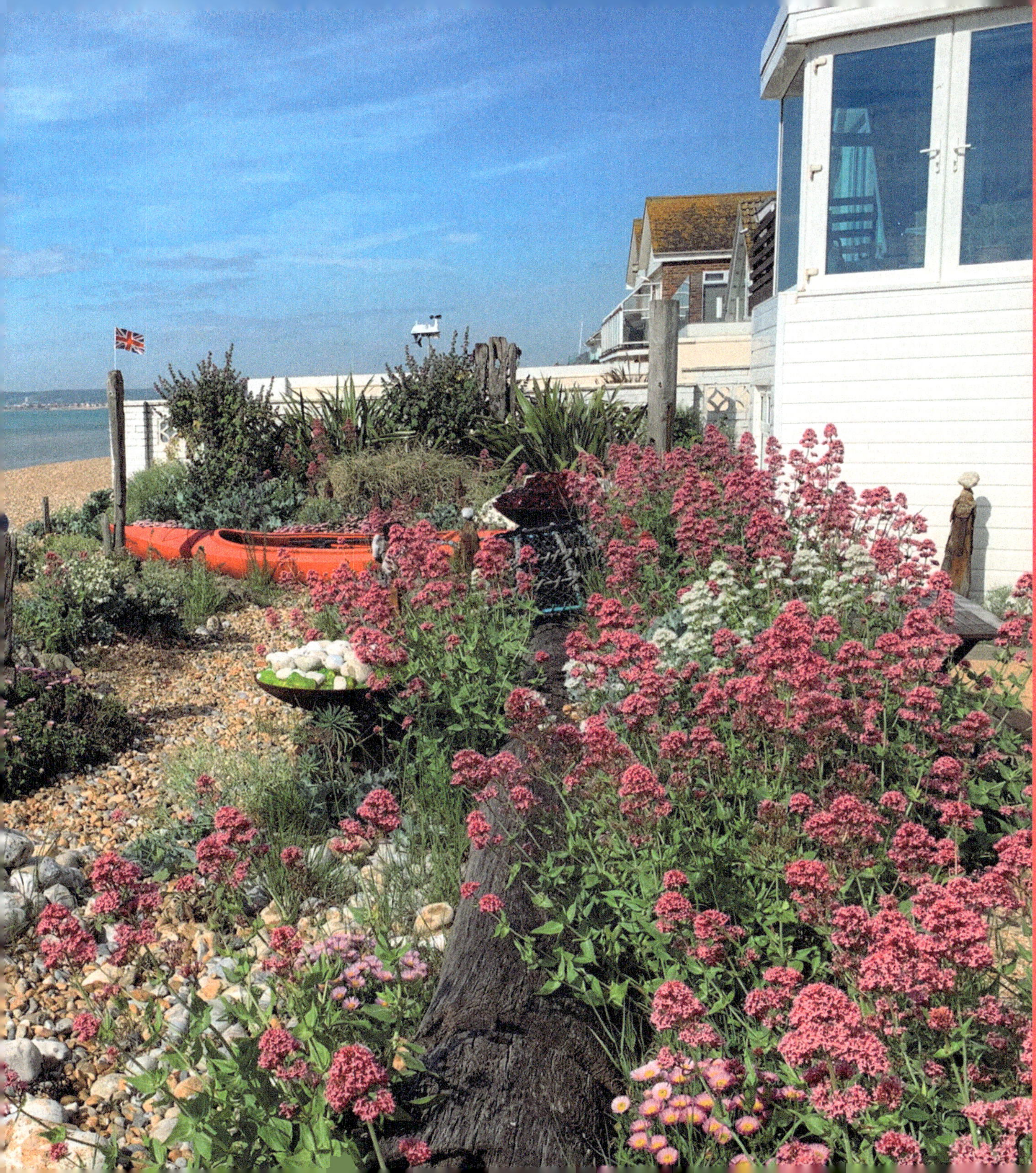

'Sculpting my garden is a breath of fresh air. I add bits I collect and evolve with the garden'

John, who is an accomplished sculptor with a background in theatrics and film making, thrives on creating a garden with a surreal theatrical theme.

The theatrical elements are clear and the mix of glass, wood and metal shows how material choice can lend a unique and particularly creative edge to coastal garden designs.

John's use of different types and colours of glass is wonderful - bright and strategically placed around the garden to create a fantastic link between areas. Blues and reds draw your eye and the uranium yellow glass glows amongst the planting to create a very surreal effect.

One surprising highlight is the lowly dandelion which does well here and gives John nostalgic memories of his younger years growing up in Manchester.

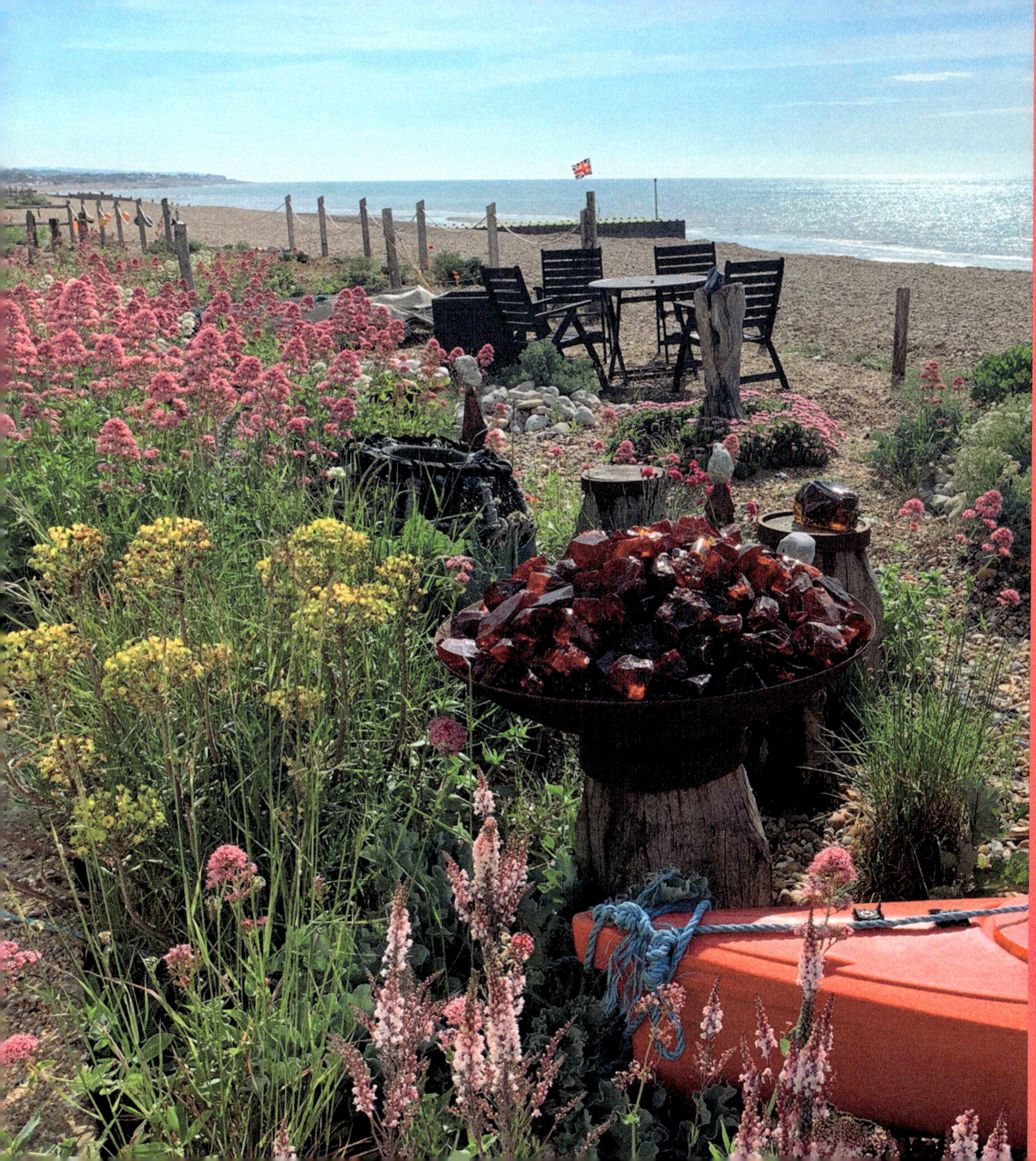

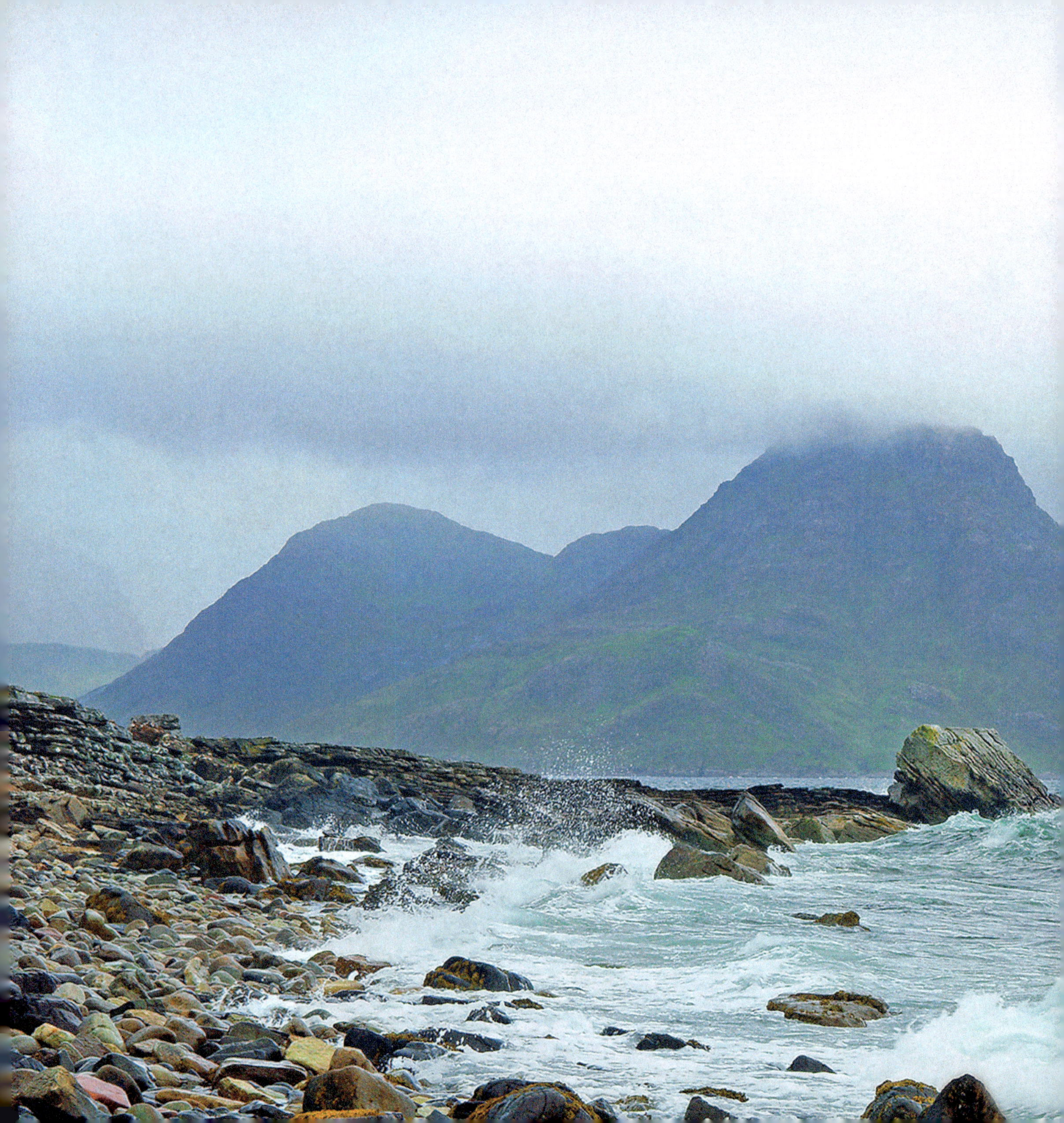

Becca Duncan
www.blossominggardens.co.uk

SCOTLAND

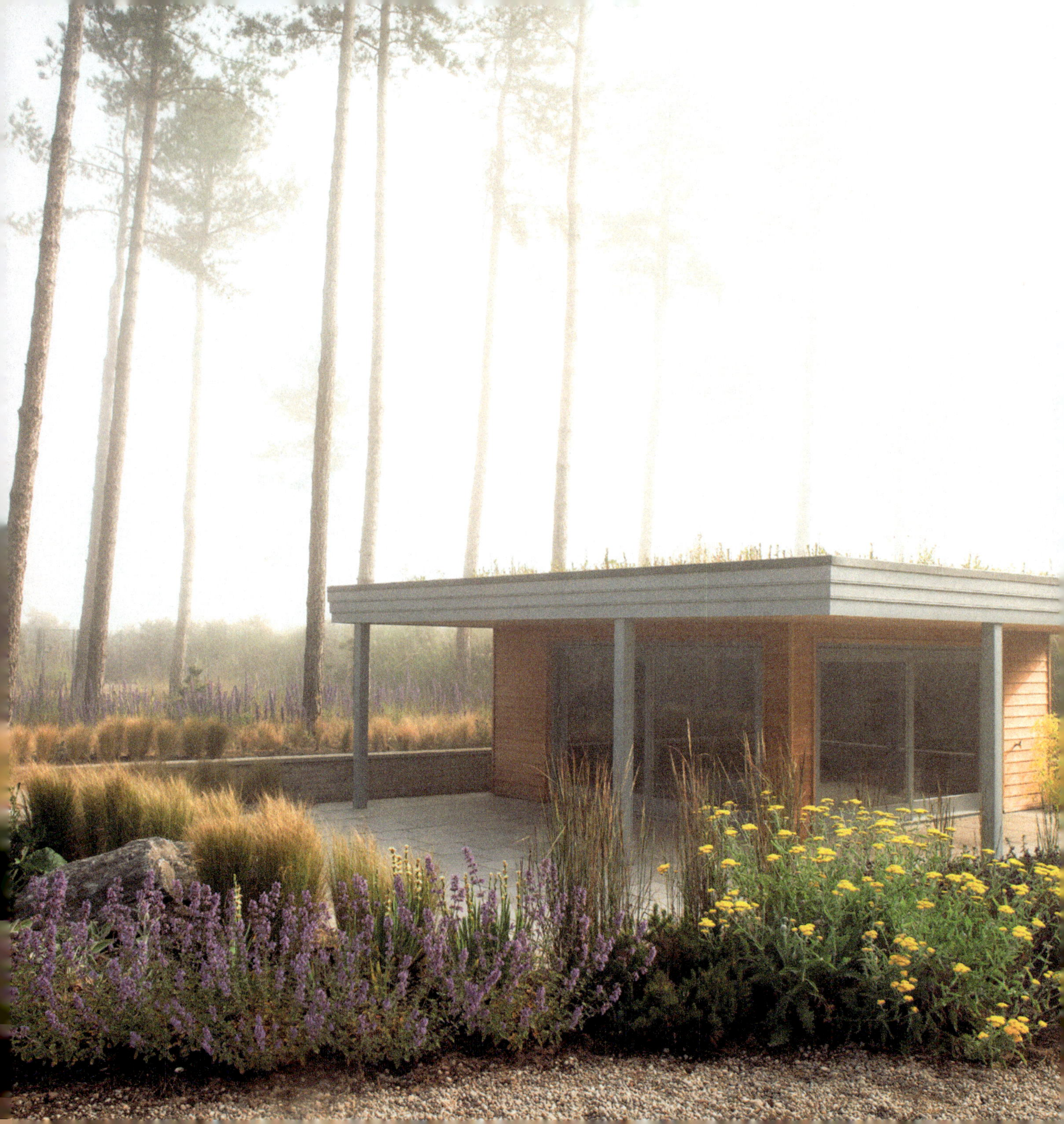

Garden Location...

The owners of this newly built beach front property in East Lothian were looking to create a very natural garden that blended in with the surrounding landscape. It was to be a space where their family could relax. With windows that extended from floor to ceiling, framing beautiful views from the house was also key.

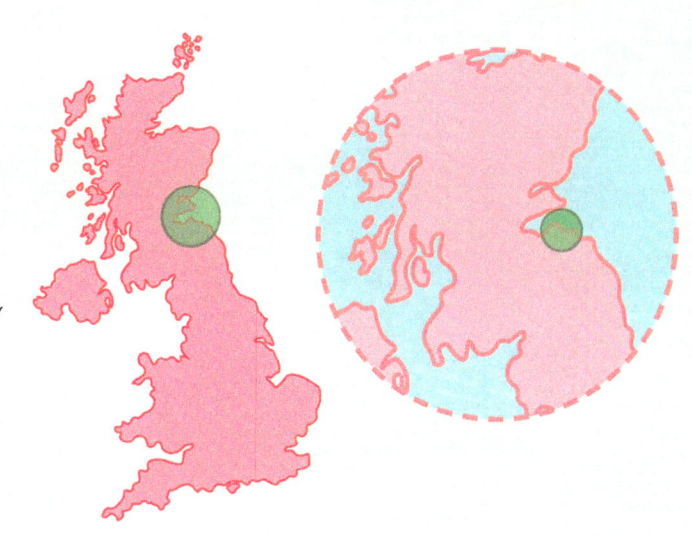

The 'beach hut' and sunken garden provide a sheltered spot for outdoor dining, as well as offering some privacy from passers-by on the coastal path along the back boundary of the garden.

Sand berms with marram grass (*Ammophila arenaria*) form a very natural edge along the neighbouring boundaries of the property. These are covered in self-seeded wild flowers, such as the blue spires of viper's-bugloss (*Echium vulgare*) and yellow spires of dyer's rocket (*Reseda luteola*) through the summer months. The sand berms are also perfect for buffering the coastal winds.

Meandering paths were formed with beach pebbles, linking the garden to the bay beyond.

There are plenty of beautiful tall pines, hawthorns, wild roses, geraniums, verbascums, yarrow, sea kale and other wildflowers and grasses growing in the surrounding coastal area in similar conditions. These and the low mounding shapes and glaucus foliage of the plants informed the designer's planting choices.

Hawthorns (Crataegus coccinea) were chosen as the perfect screen and windbreak and for their beautiful spring blossom and autumn berries.

The single flowers of Rosa 'Kew Gardens' flower through the summer and are lightly fragrant, which is noticeable as you step out of the house.

Low mounding evergreen Pinus mugo and Pinus nigra were planted through the borders to tie in with the taller, existing Pinus nigra surrounding the property.

In reference to the curving bays and contouring sand dunes that formed the stunning coastline beyond the garden, a layout of winding paths and mounded borders run all the way through the garden.

Meandering paths were formed with beach pebbles, linking the garden to the bay beyond. Path edging was not used so as to create a very natural, flowing effect.

Large rocks, similar to those found on the beach, were placed through the borders to strengthen the connection with the surrounding coastline.

Hawthorns were chosen as the perfect screen and windbreak for their beautiful spring blossom and berries.

As we are confronted with the challenges of climate change, it will become increasingly important to work with the natural conditions.

The perennials, sub-shrubs and grasses were planted from small pots into the existing sandy substrate in early spring and were not watered in, so were completely dependent on the local conditions to get established. The idea behind this was that it would force them to be tougher plants with extensive root systems perfectly adapted to the conditions.

As we are confronted with the challenges of climate change, it will become increasingly important to work with the prevailing conditions.

Despite the hostile conditions and the minimal watering, the perennials and sub-shrubs became established surprisingly quickly. They were generally smaller in size than they may have been had they been grown in a rich loamy soil. The perennials, such as yarrow (*Achillea* 'moonshine') and catmint (*Nepeta racemosa* 'walker's low') flowered prolifically throughout the summer and into the autumn. Many of these plants keep their structure through the winter, so there should be plenty to see throughout the year.

Mexican feather grass (*Nasella tennuisima*), golden oats (*Stipa gigantea*), feather reed grass (*Calamagrostis x acutiflora* 'overdam') and nest moor grass (*Sesleria nitida*) play to the windy conditions and ripple through the borders, much like the waves of the sea.

Perennials and sub-shrubs such as greater sea kale (*Crambe cordifolia*) with it's sea spray of flowers, mullein (*Verbascum* 'gainsborough'), rosemary-leaved cotton lavender (*Santolina* 'Edward Bowles'), lamb's ears (*Stachys byzantina* 'big ears'), Russian sage (*Perovskia* 'Blue Spire') and fragrant lavender (*Lavendula x intermedia* 'seal') have beautiful glaucus, textured foliage even when they are not in flower.

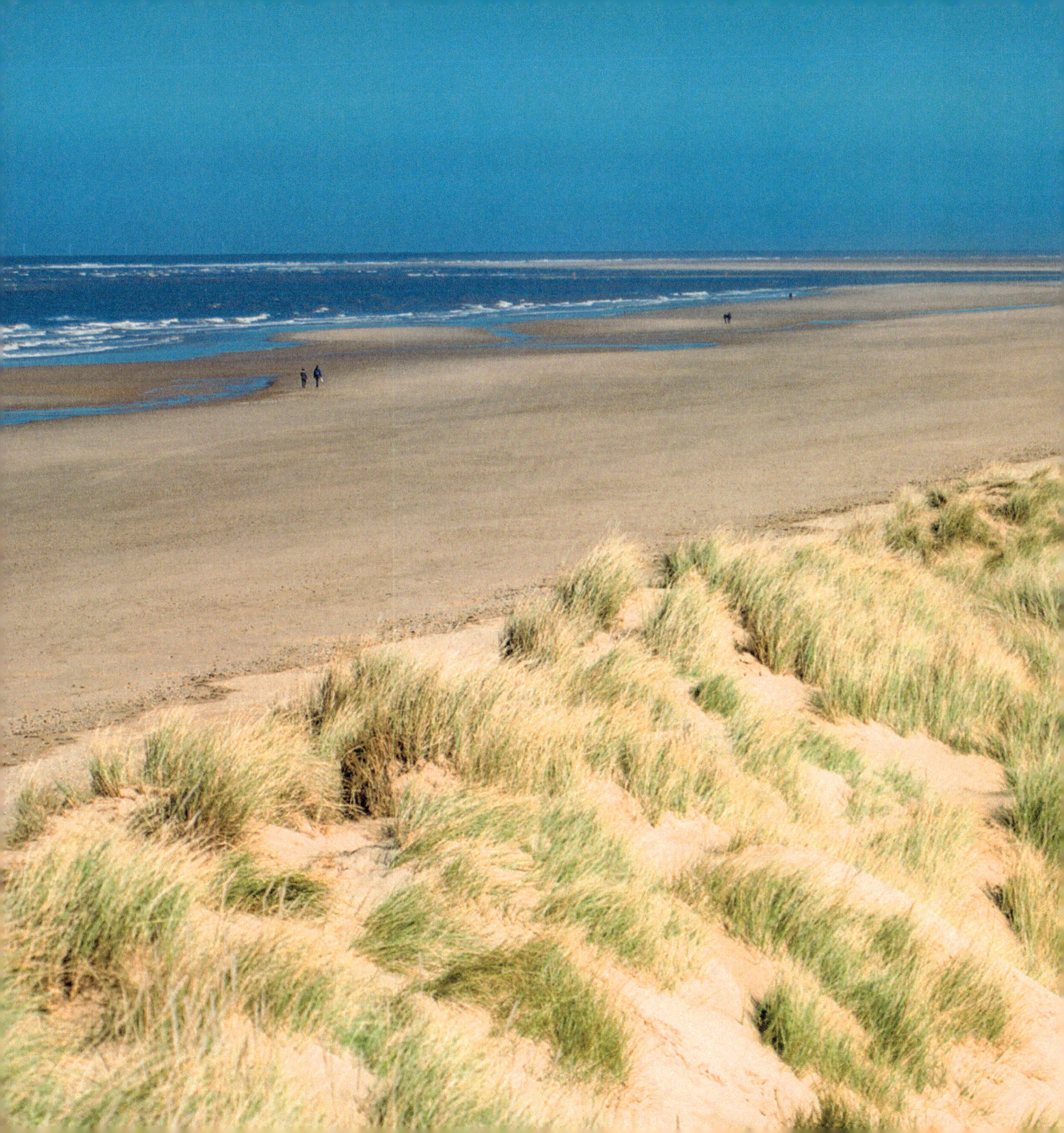

Sue Townsend
www.suetownsendgardendesign.co.uk

EAST ANGLIA

Garden Location...

The rainfall in East Anglia is the lowest in the country and the vast majority of the soil is pure sand which allows for a lovely variety of drought-tolerant plants.

Three existing silver birch trees mark the front of the property but needed underplanting with domes of pines and grasses to give more privacy.

To frame the side section of the house, a Swedish whitebeam (Sorbus intermedia 'Brouwers') was planted, which provides berries and flowers for insects and birds and can cope well with coastal conditions.

This contemporary eco holiday home is in a very exposed location on the top of a cliff overlooking the North Sea. Winds are strong, salt-laden and very cold in the winter.

The clients wanted a low maintenance family garden which connected naturally to the local environment and beach below. On the side facing the sea they wanted a lawn area, a trampoline and planting to give a little privacy. Informal paths and a secluded seating area were requested at the front of the house.

The feel of the beach was brought into the garden by using locally sourced pebbles of differing sizes. Pebbles are great for allowing rain to filter through to the sandy soil and plants.

We planted native wild species such as bladder campion (*Silene vulgaris*), sea kale (*Crambe maritima*) and marram grass (*Ammophila arenaria*), which were added as plug plants.

Sawn sandstone stepping stones set in gravel now meander to the front door and around the garden to provide easy access and allow rainfall to percolate the ground.

Drought-tolerant plants were chosen to add texture, colour and movement in the wind, whilst also helping to stabilise the sandy slope.

Grasses, fennel (*Foeniculum vulgare*) and *Verbena bonariensis* were the perfect choice for softening the fence and wall and planted alongside a hedge of *Olearia traversii*.

In the seating area, a silvergrass (*Miscanthus*) hedge was introduced to give privacy and the area surrounded by textural planting for year-round structure and food for wildlife.

Further towards the centre of the front garden, a West Himalayan birch (*Betula utilis var jacquemontii*) was planted as a focal point and uplit with subtle garden lighting. New trees of silver birch, pines and sorbus were added to reflect those growing on nearby heathland.

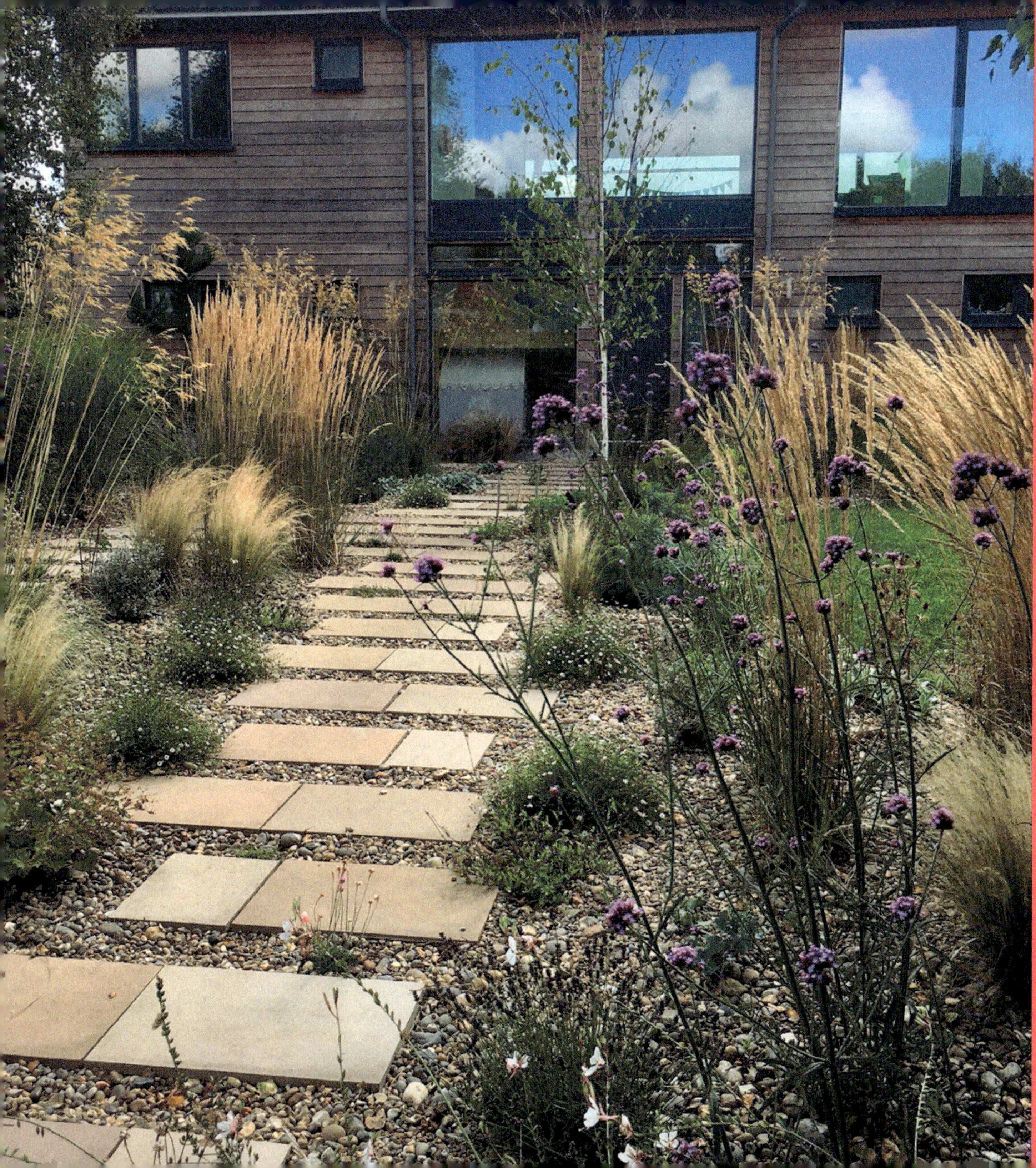

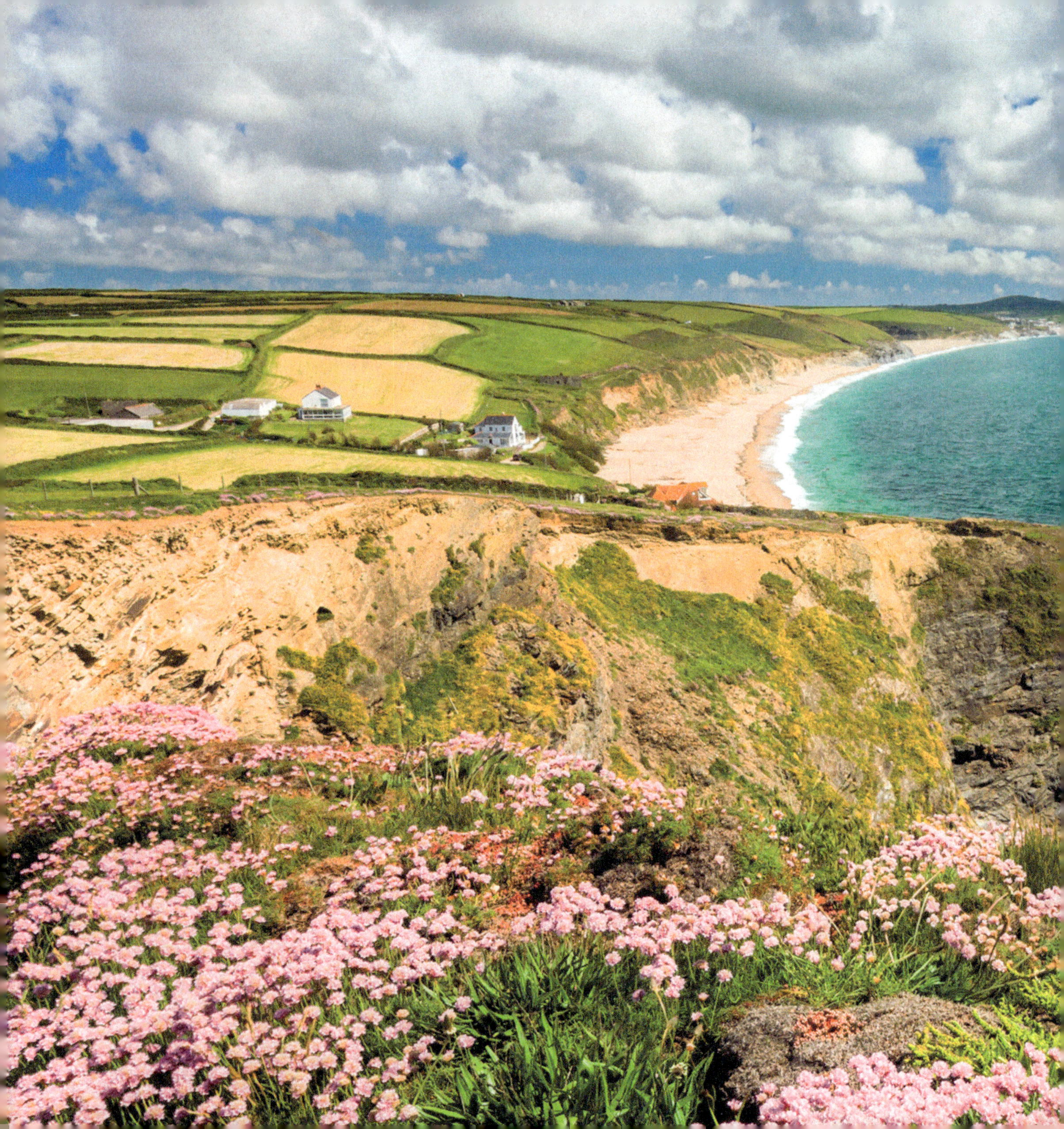

Kim Parish
www.landscapesofdistinction.co.uk

SOUTH WEST

Garden Location...

Cornwall is situated on the southwest tip of England and forms its own peninsula, encompassing 697km (433 miles) of a very varied coastline.

In close proximity to the sea, temperatures in this region are warm in the summer and mild in the winter. Rainfall is frequent and heavy allowing for luxuriant vegetation, especially in more sheltered areas.

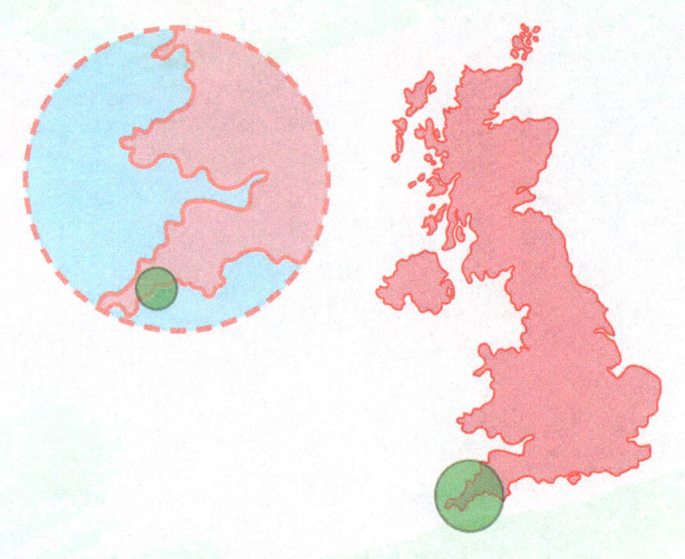

Our design had to maximise the use of the space, taking the weather into account, and create a haven for the clients, who wanted the plants to be the stars in their design.

Exposed to salty winds from the southwest and west and with high annual rainfall, this garden had to be carefully planned.

Our garden is situated on the south coast on the Roseland Peninsula. The south coast is fairly sheltered, edged by the English Channel, and has several areas which are more sub-tropical.

Exposed to salty winds from the southwest and west and with a high annual rainfall, this garden had to be carefully planned.

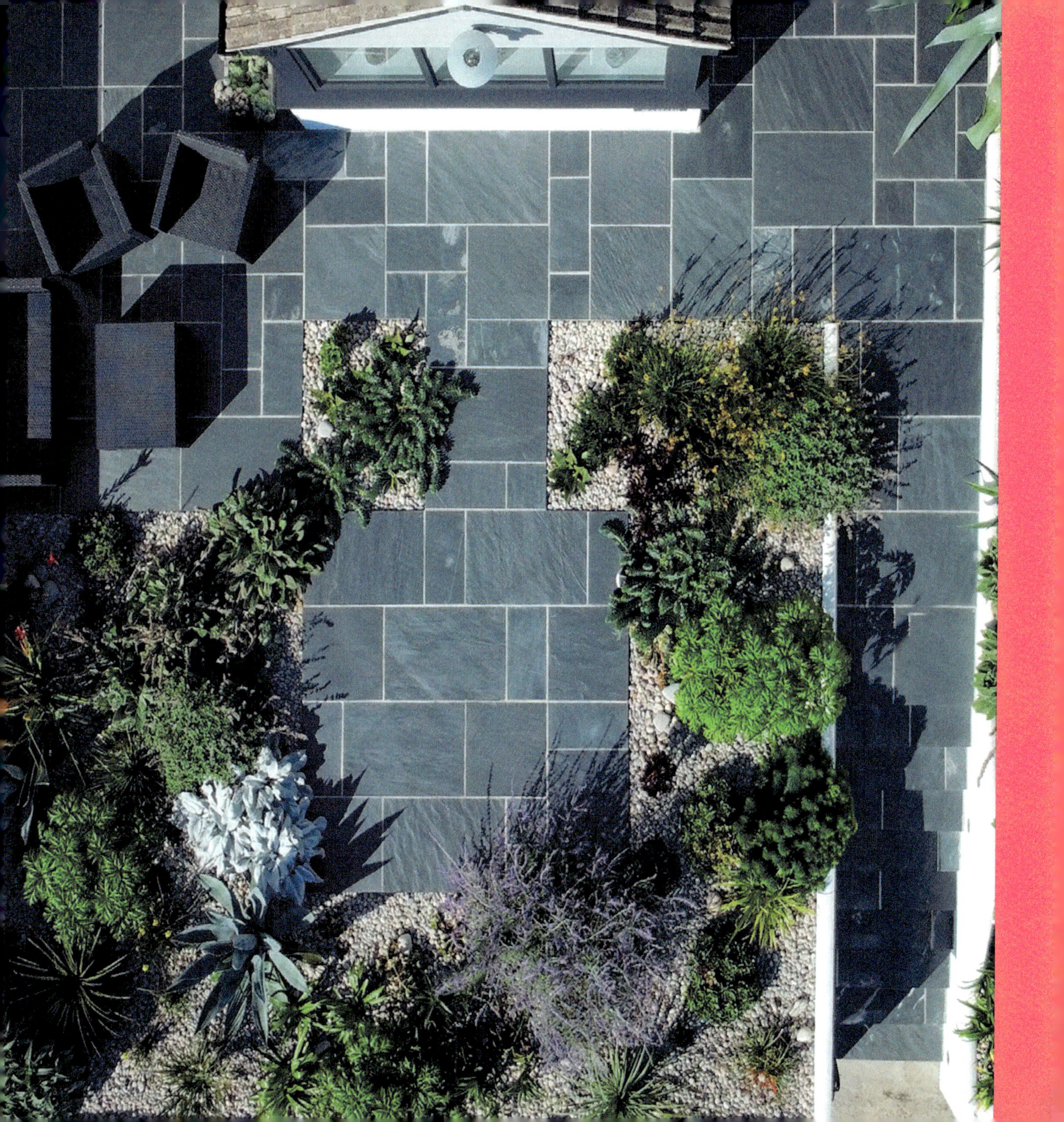

Our clients wanted a tropical garden with a coastal undertone and are very keen on exotic plants, especially succulents. The garden has a view of the sea and the clients wanted to ensure that none of the plants would block any views, either for themselves or their neighbour.

Most of the plants chosen would not exceed the height of the wall, but a few statement plants; giant viper's-bugloss (*Echium pininana*) and conebushes (*Leucadendron* 'Safari Sunset') were used to add height without interrupting the view.

We were able to relocate the client's large century plant (*Agave americana*) and we dramatically thinned out the existing African lily (*Agapanthus africanus*), which is so successful in Cornwall that it can be considered invasive. Re-planting a single clump through a membrane allowed us to limit its spread, and we introduced a second variety to extend the interest.

An array of succulents, such as *Aeonium, Agave, Aloe, Bulbine and Echeveria*, created a striking display and evergreen structure was added by including trunkless tropical plants, bromeliads and grasses, chosen to create privacy at the edge of the garden.

The hard landscaping materials needed to be carefully considered, so as to complement the materials already in situ inside the property and create a seamless transition from inside to out, whilst giving a lovely contemporary feel.

Grey slate pavers were the perfect choice - modern and tough, built to withstand the high rainfall and non-marking, unlike some other materials.

Low growing evergreen succulent perennials such as *Euphorbia*, *Sedum* and *Echeveria* were the perfect creeping plants to spread and soften the paving edges.

Aeonium 'Velour'

We designed two separate seating areas for the clients, each with its own benefits, giving them the option to choose the best setting depending on the weather.

One was built in the most sheltered position, away from the wind and taking advantage of the sunniest spot in the garden. The small central area is a little more exposed but offers sea views.

Substantially heavy furniture was chosen so that we could avoid it blowing around and causing damage to the site during windy conditions.

We chose a pebble mulch instead of a traditional bark mulch, because the high winds would scatter the bark - the pebbles will stay put.

The property was being renovated and the implementation of the front garden was to follow on from the completion of this work. Our design layout was dictated by access to the property and road, prevailing winds, shelter, sun and views.

We managed to create a stunning design, incorporating all the elements requested by our clients including a smooth 'indoor-outdoor' transition, seating areas in the perfect spots to make the best of the site & sea views and, above all, for the chosen plants to be the stars of the show.

Re-using some of the client's original plants is always nice to be able to do. Creating a beautiful garden which is used year-round in a place with challenging and changing weather has been very satisfying and we are all thrilled with the result.

IVY & WHYTE

05

Our work flow through the design process is very much creating a rapport with our clients and finding out exactly what they want from their coastal garden. This includes all the fun bits as well as the not-so-fun functional elements such as housing household waste bins. It is exciting to harness the local environment. The following design is a good example of this. One of the most appealing elements of designing a coastal garden is letting your imagination run wild. Everything from driftwood to metal sculptures find their way into our designs and we use plants that work in the environment they are in. Based in Kent and Sussex, we have plenty of coast to play with and gather inspiration from.

Garden Location...

Our clients were keen to add some drama to their garden, which is right on the seafront, just behind a sea wall. The house is 4 storeys high with their kitchen/living area at the top.

They wanted to be enticed down to their garden from the top floor, so we were tasked with creating a really unique garden that looked just as stunning from above as it did at ground level.

It was a very exciting but challenging project as the site was very exposed to the elements and we had to think about it from many angles.

When designing a garden we start off by considering the location and the surroundings, taking any views and permanent structures into account.

In this coastal garden there was a concrete sea barrier wall in the background, and as the house is a contemporary new build we thought it would work well to bring that element into the garden by re-creating the concrete structure as a statement sculpture.

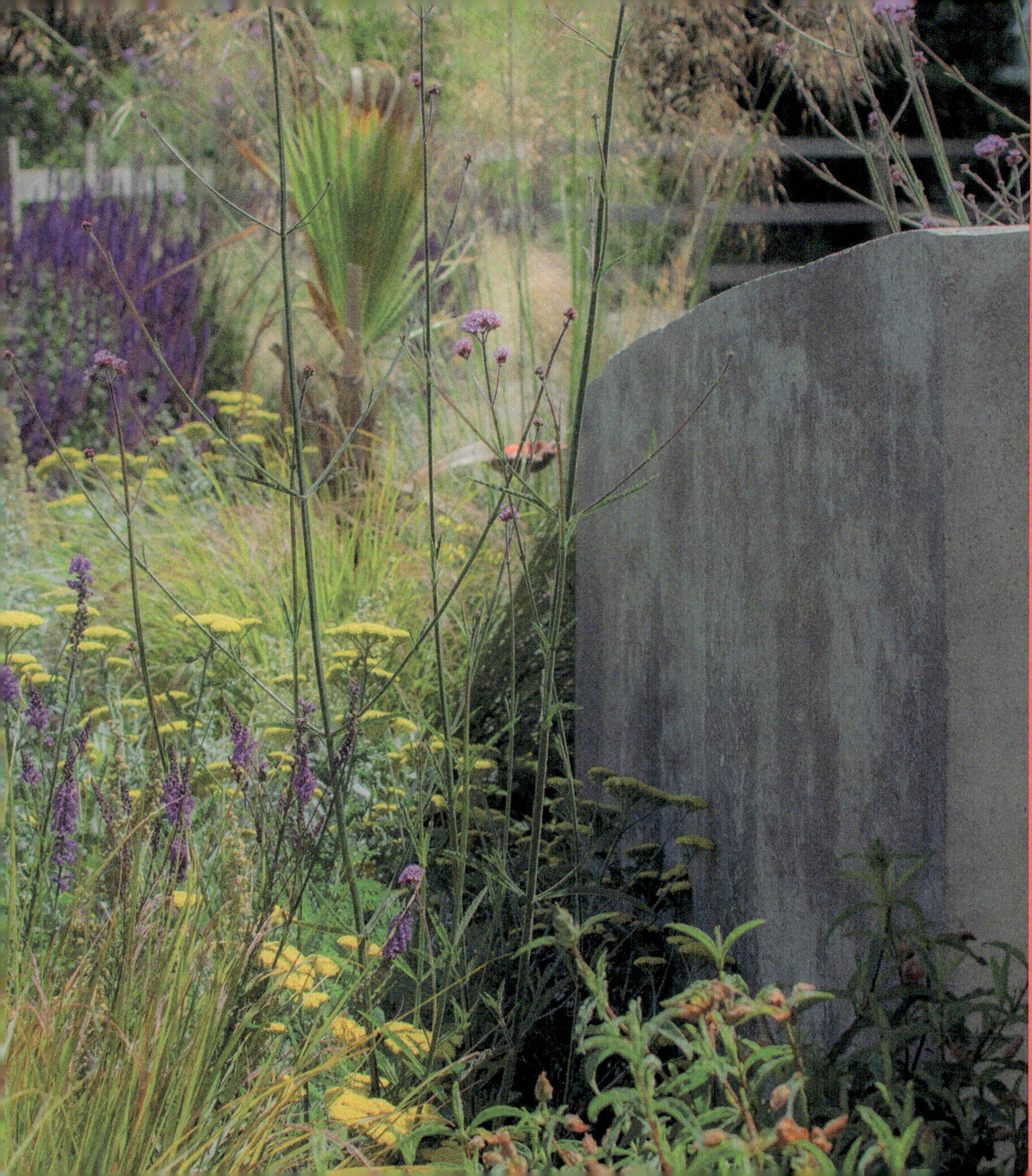

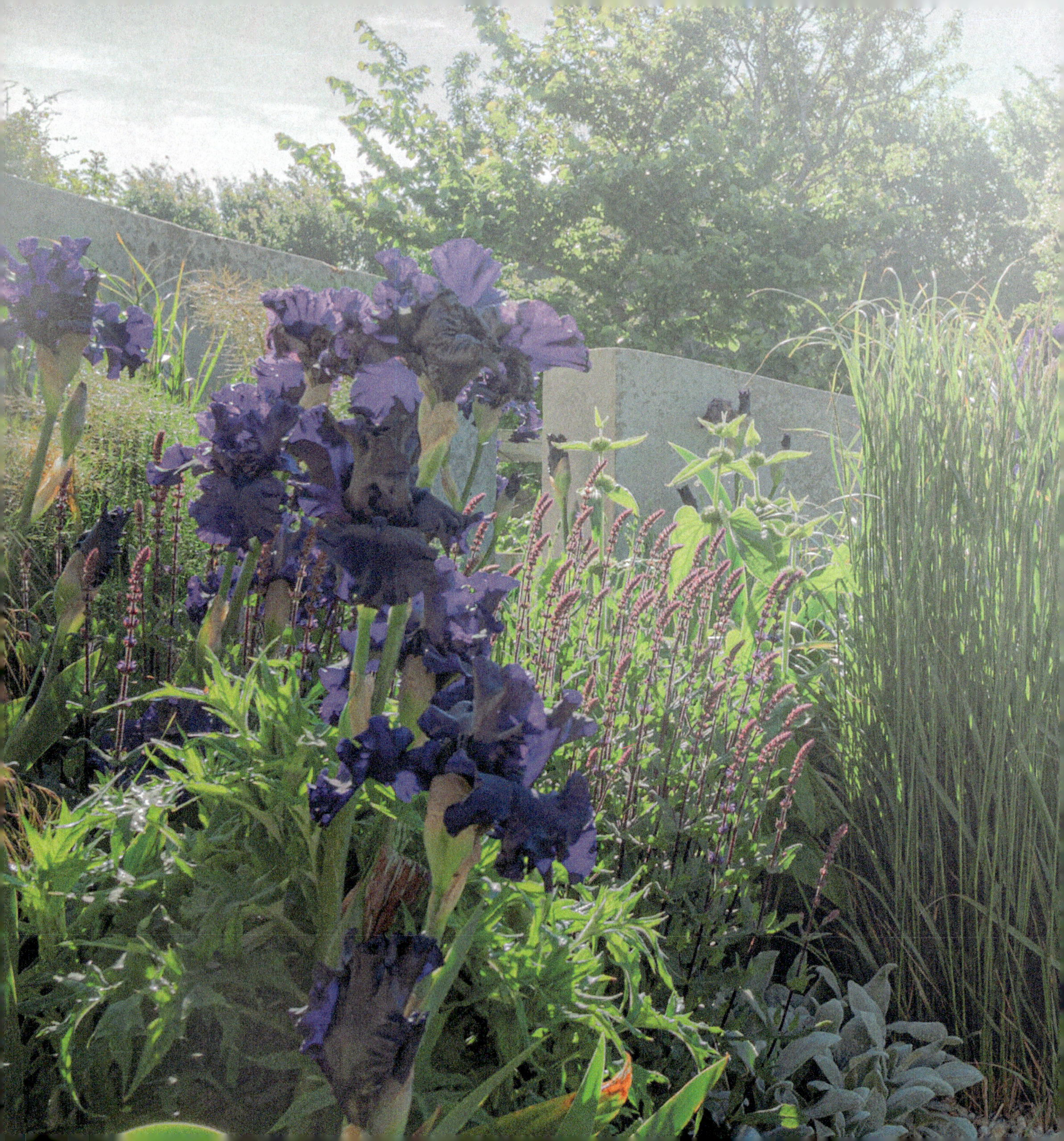

We didn't want to create just a straight concrete wall as we felt that this would be too imposing. The setting is informal, located next to a stream and backing onto a wildflower meadow, so we created two large curved concrete sculptures, each mirroring the other, and softened them with planting which reflected the surrounding areas.

The two sculptures start high and then gradually curve round down to ground level. We designed a selection of windows to sit within the concrete to frame specific parts of the garden. These concrete sculptures really brought the requested drama.

We wanted to keep the planting really natural to link in with the surrounding areas and chose a range of plants with a variety of different textures from spiky *Phormium* to soft grasses which adds more interest to the garden.

We chose plants of varying heights including lots of grasses and perennials which would sway in the wind. Low growing plants such as *stachys* and *geranium* creep along the borders.

Planting was added to all sides of the sculptures which really softens them.

All planting had to be carefully considered to ensure that all the varieties could withstand harsh, salty conditions as the garden is situated just a few metres from the beach. Drought-tolerant, silver-leaved plants played a large part in the final design.

We chose a vibrant palette - mainly purple and yellows, because they really bounce off each other well. Many grass varieties were included, along with thistle-style plants such as *eryngium* and *echinops*, because they are fantastic sculptural plants which look just as incredible in the winter months as they do in the summer.

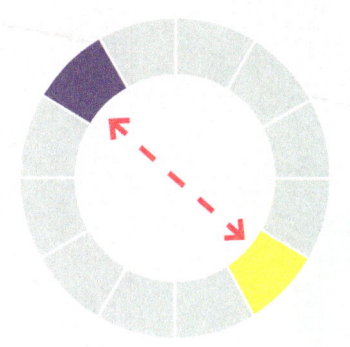

When choosing the perfect shrubs and trees, pleached hollies *(Ilex aquifolium)* were a good choice as they can withstand harsh conditions.

We wanted to finish the beds off with pebbles to add to the beach effect and chose gravel of different gradients to make it look more naturalistic.

The beds are edged with corten steel to keep the line neat and give the lawn a nice crisp, curved edge.

DESIGN

84

YOUR OWN

Amelanchier tree to soften the hardness of the wall and screen

Irregularly placed planting within the gravel as is found along the coast

Golden tone gravel similar to that found on the seafront

Wood-effect porcelain paving to mimic coastal boardwalks

Woven willow screening to complement natural materials and tones of the garden

Subtle tone painted fence to complement silver and green planting scheme

Different pavers to create the feeling of a zone, almost like an outdoor carpet

MATERIALS AND FEATURES

06

What materials make you think 'coastal'? What makes them coastal and what do you like about them? These are good questions to ask yourself when choosing the types of materials to introduce to your scheme. When we look at certain materials they evoke certain feelings and give us a sense of something and that is different for everyone. What do *you* like?

From metal posts to sea groynes, whimsical signs to stripy beach huts, there is so much inspiration to be gathered from spending time in the place you are trying to replicate. You may be looking to create a natural coastal garden or a more fun beach feel - immerse yourself in your ideal space and in images in magazines and online to get a really good feel for what will work for you.

In this chapter, we'll consider different materials such as shingle, steel and wood and how best to use them. One of the most enjoyable aspects of designing a coastal garden is the freedom it gives you to use different features and here we'll focus on some of our favourites.

METAL

Found in natural beach settings, metal can be a powerful element within a garden design and is a versatile material that could be used as an aesthetic sculptural object, a retaining wall or a water feature.

You could choose to use aluminium, corten steel, mild steel or stainless steel. It is highly recommended to research the durability, rust damage and visual effect the coastal elements may have on them over time. Corten is one to be careful of if you have particular direct exposure to salt.

Aluminium is usually powder-coated and commonly used for pergola frames. It is a good material to use in a contemporary coastal garden. A metal such as corten steel will rust over time, which works well in a natural and rustic coastal garden.

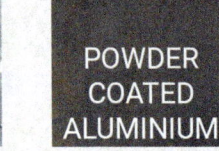

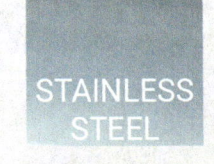

- WROUGHT IRON
- GALVANISED STEEL
- CORTEN STEEL
- COPPER
- PATTERN SCREEN
- STAINLESS STEEL
- MILD STEEL
- POWDER COATED ALUMINIUM
- CORRUGATED IRON

Powder-coated aluminium sculptures are relatively low-maintenance. This is especially advantageous in coastal gardens, where constant exposure to salt and moisture can accelerate wear and tear. The cube's sharp lines and distinct shape can serve as a striking focal point in the garden, contrasting with the softer, more organic forms typically found in coastal landscapes.

Steel shipping containers add an industrial look to the coast and can be playfully painted with endless colour combinations

Railway sleeper walkway adds a natural and weathered look to the space

Vertical railway sleeper walls complement the walkway

Large palm trees dotted throughout – a great plant tolerant of strong coastal winds

Large boulders add a sculptural interest and act as seating spots

Fishing rope used as barriers

Concrete can be found all along the coast - in the sea walls, promenades, flood defences and boat ramps.

It's a very versatile material that suits more contemporary styles. It is in itself very minimalistic with clean lines and a unique texture that can be easily manipulated.

Concrete is a very practical solution for retaining walls and free-standing structures. If you're looking to have a very eco-friendly garden you may want to research sustainable concrete that releases less carbon dioxide in production as this is the only downside to this industrial material.

CONCRETE

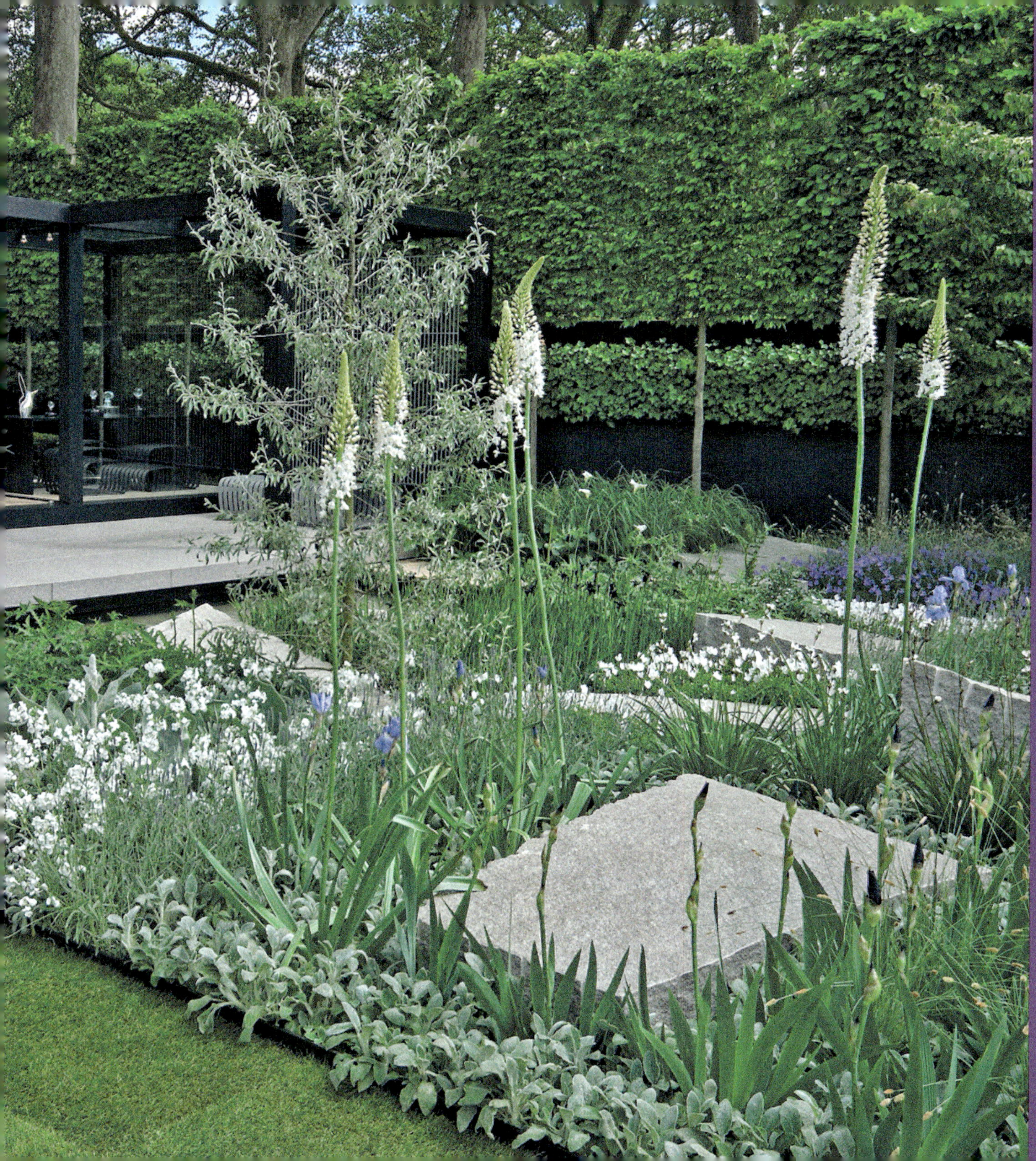

GRAVEL AND COBBLES

Pebble beaches are a big inspiration for gravel coastal gardens. They can be replicated by having gravel or cobble pathways. For best coastal results, a mixture of sizes need to be used throughout the garden and in and around plants to give it a natural look.

Drought resistant gardens are often gravel-covered. Dry gardens and drought-tolerant plants are great considerations for areas that get a lot of sun and for those people who have limited time and are unable to commit to watering every day during the summer.

Gravel is a porous material which helps to promote efficient drainage. This helps prevent waterlogging in the garden, which is crucial in coastal zones where excess moisture can be a common issue.

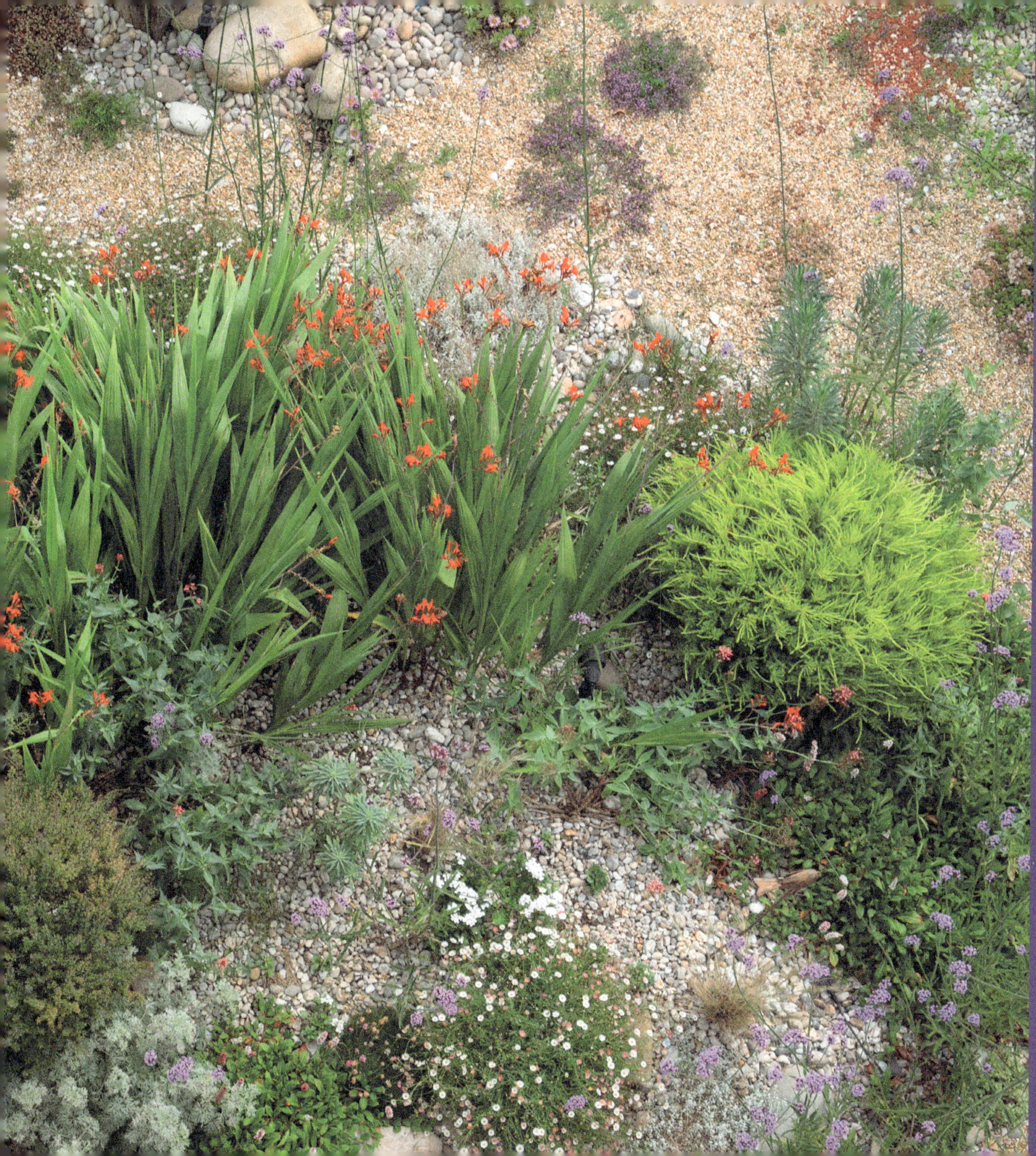

SLATE

FLAT COBBLES

LIMESTONE

VARIED GRAVEL

QUARTS GRAVEL

WHITE MARBLE

FLINT GRAVEL

SANDY

COMPRESSED GRANITE

FLINT PEBBLES

RIPPLED COBBLES

GOLDEN BUFF

98

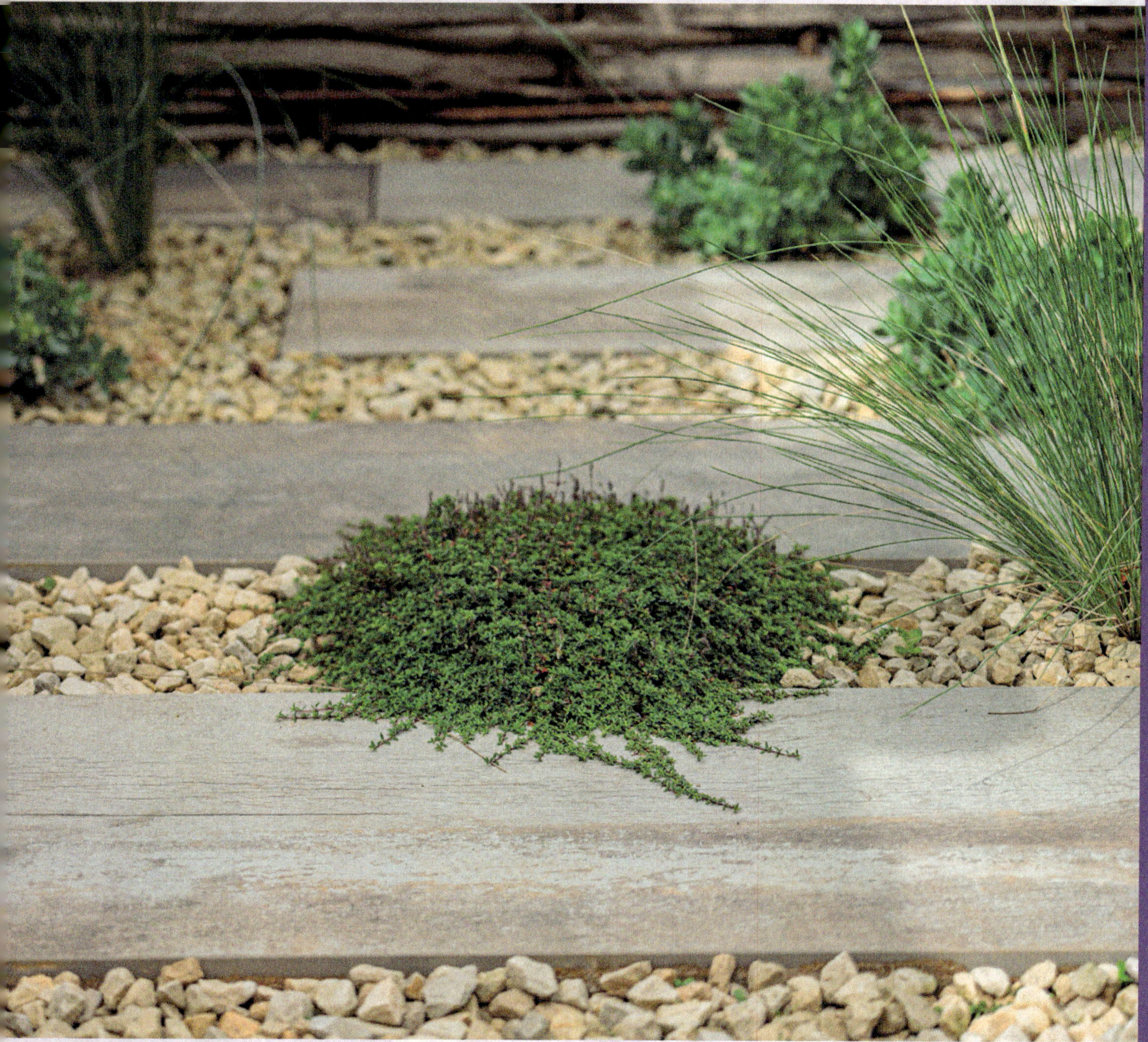

TIMBER

Wood is incredibly versatile and can be used in countless ways within a coastal garden design. Weathered wood within a sea of shingle instantly takes you to the coast.

One of the major features of a coastal view is the unmistakeable presence of sea groynes - large, striking structures that look as though they've been there since the dawn of time. They can be rather expensive to buy and hard to get hold of, but wooden sleepers can be the perfect alternative.

Streamlined and slightly less domineering within a smaller space, the sleeper has the desired rustic look and can be used vertically or horizontally within a garden design to create an instant beach feel.

Traditionally used to lay rail tracks on, the rustic look and manageable size of a wooden sleeper can be a brilliant addition to your coastal garden. You could create a boardwalk with them, build raised beds or use them to separate areas within your design. You can build structural sculptures to bring height and interest or create steps for access between different levels.

OAK	CEDAR	ACCOYA
CHESTNUT	PINE	CHARRED
HAZEL	JATOBA	IROKO

Timber has a warm and natural appearance that complements the coastal landscape, but it can easily be customised to fit the specific design requirements of the space: stained or painted to match or contrast with the surrounding environment or other garden features.

Spaced plank paving walkway similar to a coastal boardwalk

Reclaimed sea groynes with a rustic texture are a focal point

Staggered groynes placed in front of a clear view allow hints of the vista

Large terracotta pots act as sculptures in the garden

COVER

Our British weather is traditionally up and down, and you'll often experience an unexpected day of chilly wind, driving rain or belting heat. It's always worth being prepared, so don't forget to bear this in mind when designing your garden.

In a coastal garden, weather changes can be extreme – the wind from the coast can be salty and harsh and everyone knows what a day on the beach without adequate sun protection can do to your skin.

Consider where the sun falls at particular times of day, how and when you will use the garden, and whether delicate plants need protection.

Maybe you need to introduce some cover to protect you from salty air or rainy weather. Are there options for shade if guests do not like to be sat in direct sunlight? Outdoor blinds can be installed so as to respond to the change in sun direction when necessary. Perhaps the idea of sitting outside regardless of rain appeals to you. If so, you may want to consider this when designing your seating area.

Options for cover within gardens are limitless – a sail will give an instant coastal-feel - held aloft above a seating area, it can give you access to a much-needed cooler space on a hot day. If you prefer a more formal look, consider a pergola – made of steel, aluminium or wood, it can be strung with lights or softened with a climbing plant.

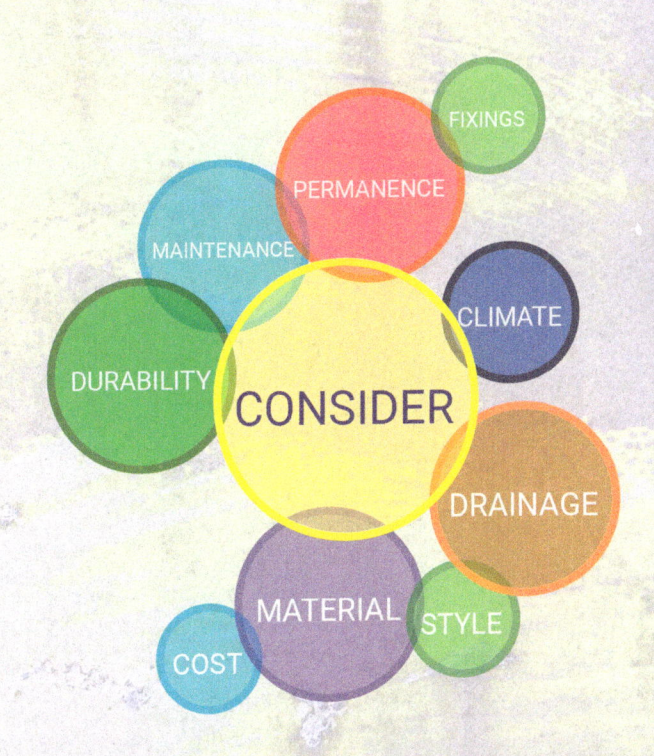

CONSIDER: FIXINGS, PERMANENCE, MAINTENANCE, CLIMATE, DURABILITY, DRAINAGE, COST, MATERIAL, STYLE

105

WINDBREAK

Screening areas of your garden can have many different effects and be used for different purposes, such as separating areas of a garden into "rooms" or for protection. Windbreaks are invaluable and versatile objects which ultimately protect. Perhaps you need to ensure that delicate planting is cosseted from the elements – especially in a coastal garden where salty, harsh, windy conditions prevail, or maybe you just need protection for yourself so that you can enjoy your garden without being blown away.

Coastal gardens can be breezy and even if you live inland, you'll have experienced unwelcome windy weather at one time or another which can negatively affect an afternoon of entertaining or relaxation in your outdoor space.

A semi-permeable windbreak is ideal. A windbreak with around 50-60% permeability such as perforated panels and slatted posts allows some air to flow through whilst mitigating the full force of the wind. This helps to reduce the wind's intensity, providing a more balanced and moderated microclimate within the garden.

A windbreak or two may be the perfect solution, so what are the options? You may choose to use soft forms such as privet hedging or weaved willow or hazel screens which are easy to install and perfect for giving a natural look, or a line of pleached trees which can give a more formal look with extra height.

When it comes to hard forms of windbreak, you may choose to use fencing, metal screens – some can be very decorative and be a focal point in themselves, or maybe you would prefer a sculptural design using sleepers or blocks. If you like the idea of a more solid structure, but need to soften the look, planting can play a major part.

Whichever you prefer, it's worth considering just how windy your area is. Sometimes, a solid structure such as a fence may take more damage because it has no give, whereas a hedge can tolerate a lot more movement.

SOFT WINDBREAK	HARD WINDBREAK
HEDGES	FENCING
TREES	SCULPTURES
TALL SHRUBS	WALLS
TALL PERENNIALS	BUILDINGS
TALL GRASSES	PERGOLAS
LIVING WALLS	TRELLIS/PANELS

DRIFTWOOD

Driftwood is a beautiful natural material and is a work of nature - no two pieces are the same, each having its own characteristic texture, shape and colour.

There are so many uses for driftwood in the garden. It can be used to create visual interest as a bespoke item, such as a bench, a bird box or a quirky sculpture - anything you can think of! If you're feeling rather inventive, you could even make it into a water feature. Endlessly versatile, you can place it in all manner of different ways and create a unique visual feature.

> Driftwood often carries a sense of nostalgia and connection to the sea, evoking memories of beachcombing and coastal vacations. It can infuse your garden with a sense of relaxation and serenity.

SCULPTURE

Corten steel is a very good choice for a metal sculpture - it changes colour in the rain and is very vibrant when the sun comes out. It almost looks as though it's living, with its changing rusty texture. It has a protective coating, so it's very good at standing up against the windy, salty conditions found by the coast.

There is quite a varied range of corten steel sculptures available, from birds and sea creatures to more abstract pieces. You could have one large striking piece or group several smaller pieces in a planted border to give the impression of one larger sculpture.

Stainless steel is another good metal to use for garden sculptures - its crisp, clean and reflective qualities work well in a contemporary garden. A large circular sculpture can be a stunning focal point.

Bronze sculptures work beautifully by the sea - the harsh conditions naturally weather and change the colour over time into a beautiful turquoise-green and can look really striking. A large sphere sculpture placed at the end of a garden can often be a compelling focal point.

BOULDERS

Boulders can be seen naturally occurring along rugged UK coastlines. They are striking sculptures that can really bring a coastal garden to life. They work particularly well alongside cobbles and gravel of mixed sizes, but all should be purchased rather than taken.

Work with them, laying them out individually or in groups of three.

Boulders usually have subtle colouring, and planted alongside bold colourful plants, they can offer an impressive contrast.

BEACH HUTS

Beach huts are an iconic feature of the British coast and are a great way to bring playfulness into your garden.

Simply painting a wooden shed in a bold striped pattern can emulate a beach hut and be a really striking addition to a coastal garden.

Beach hut stripes can be bright or pastel, wide or narrow - whatever works well within your own design.

SEA GROYNES

Sea groynes are wooden structures built to reduce the shift of pebbles and sand along beaches. Over time, they become weathered, giving them a unique look and texture that is desirable in a coastal garden. The small details are always interesting in sea groynes - they often have rusty nails or stones lodged in them which can bring an extra element of texture and colour.

They can be used as features within flowerbeds or paths, or as practical structures like retaining walls. These mustn't be taken from the beach, but can be purchased.

WATER FEATURES

Coastal gardens generally reflect the elements found on the shoreline - obviously the sea is the major element, and with this comes the sound of waves gently caressing the pebbles or sand.

Water features come in all shapes and sizes and are found in every style of garden. They can fit wonderfully into a coastal garden, offering the soothing sound of moving water.

The style of the water feature may differ depending on the theme and style of your garden. The use of sea groynes, metal rills and cobble waterways all link well with the coastal style. Alternatively, you could choose to buy a standalone feature of metal and spheres, which can work just as well.

The reflective surface of water features can be used strategically to mirror the sky and surrounding landscape, creating a sense of spaciousness and depth in your garden. This visual effect can make the space feel larger and more open.

Coastal plants can work well alongside a garden pond.

Rock and slate have a coastal feel and can be used to create a natural waterfall.

Great for all your amazing wildlife too.

You may question including a pond in a coastal design, but provided it is sympathetically designed, it can work really well and the inclusion of rocks or different stone adds to the drama.

PAVING SLABS

The humble paving slab is possibly the most commonly used material to create garden patios. It gives a practical solid surface and can be used to complement different styles as it is available in many different textures and colours. If you have a large area, you could possibly look at breaking up an expanse of slabs with another material - this keeps the garden looking natural and interesting.

Some examples of materials used include porcelain, yorkstone, sandstone and slate, although there are many others. It is worth visiting your local paving supplier to see all the available options.

Paving slabs are often the favoured choice as they provide a stable foundation for outdoor furniture, ensuring that tables, chairs, and loungers remain level and secure, even on uneven terrain.

Most paving slabs are designed to have a slip-resistant surface, ensuring safety for both residents and visitors.

BROWN INDIAN SANDSTONE

SMOOTH SANDSTONE

LIMESTONE

YORKSTONE

BLACK GRANITE

BLACK SLATE

INDIAN SANDSTONE

GREY BASALT

RECLAIMED YORKSTONE

BEIGE PORCELAIN

GREY PORCELAIN

WOOD EFFECT PORCELAIN

Plank paving can be a great idea for a coastal design as it complements the coastal theme by mimicking the look of boardwalks, piers, and beachfront pathways.

Wood-effect porcelain can give a strong coastal aesthetic if you place long tiles within a gravel path, or use them to guide the way through an area of plants or grass. It can also be used as a breaker if you have too much of one material or texture in an area. Wood-effect porcelain comes in a range of colours, textures, and patterns, allowing you to choose a style that complements your specific coastal garden design.

COMPOSITE DECKING

Wooden decking is used in all styles of garden and is ideal for sloping gardens where it's traditionally been used to create levels easily.

Decking has evolved from traditional wood, which does require quite high maintenance, to the more durable composite deck. Composite, although a man-made product, offers a variety of colours and natural wood textures, which can give a modern feel to the garden.

From a design perspective, composite is a very versatile, long-lasting and neat-looking product which has the ability to break up zones in the garden. If you're planning on extending out at a height, it is always advisable to check with your local authority as to limitations.

Composite decking has a longer lifespan than wooden decking. It can last 25-30 years or more, whereas natural wooden decking may require replacement or extensive refurbishment sooner. Another benefit of composite decking is that it is impervious to rot and decay, ensuring the integrity of your deck over time.

Composite decking is manufactured to be consistent in size and quality. It doesn't have the variations, knots, or imperfections often found in natural wood, resulting in a smoother and more even surface.

PAVERS

Clay pavers are natural and sustainable, made from raw materials of clay and water. They are incredibly durable and weather resistant, so are perfect to use by the coast.

They are slimmer than a normal brick so are quite elegant, and work well to break up a patio to add more interest. They are full of character with their different earthy tones, and can really complement the natural tones of other coastal materials, such as pebbles.

Pavers can be laid in different patterns to add interest, formality and dynamism to the garden

Darker pavers in a herringbone pattern create a new zone

Paving zone edged with running bond pattern

Reclaimed clay pavers provide varying tones

COLOUR

07

There are so many ways to get creative with colour in your garden. You might want to create zones or rooms with different colour schemes, create single-colour borders, have bright and bold feature walls or one scheme for the whole garden, the opportunities are endless.

When choosing your colour scheme, the first step is to decide if you'd like a minimalistic/contemporary style, created by using between 1 and 3 colours, or more of a naturalistic-style garden which includes lots of different colours.

Either way, it is advisable to choose one "accent" colour, defined as a bold colour used in quite small quantities to add impact and interest. This is an effective approach when considering planting schemes and often tends to be a bright colour like orange, blue or red. The predominant colour range within a garden is often green tones so having a different colour that bursts through this always adds excitement.

COLOUR COMBINATIONS

WARM VS. COOL

The colour wheel is split in half, with one side being a collection of warm tone colours and the other, cool. Warm colours tend to be bold and powerful with cool colours being calming and not too overpowering. Warm colours often appear in tropical planting with the cooler colours being used in more traditional schemes. Whole planting schemes are often chosen by using either a warm or cool scheme.

COMPLEMENTARY

Directly opposite one another on the wheel, complementary colours can be used together to enhance the other's intensity. Using complementary colours in a planting scheme is a great way to create a bold, colourful garden display and is often why purple and yellow plants are used together in designed planting beds.

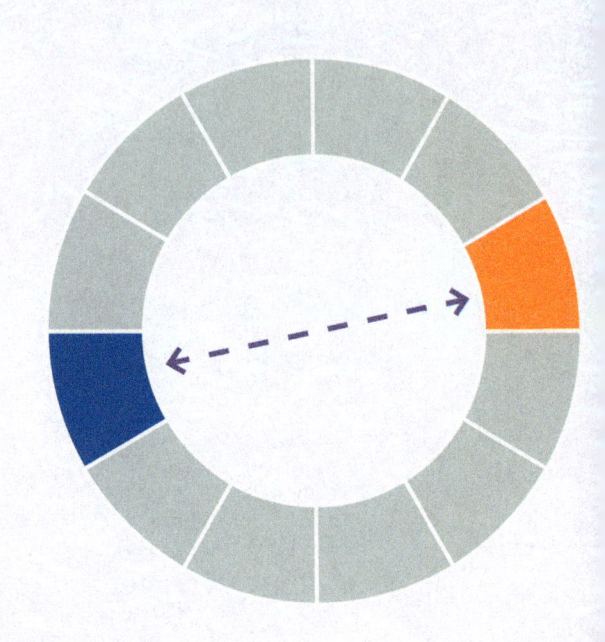

120

TRIADIC

Triadic means any three colours that are equally spaced on the colour wheel. Using these colours can form a lively palette. It is traditionally balanced so that one colour is chosen as the dominant one and the others used as accents. This is useful if you want to design a garden that is bold and colourful, but not too overpowering.

SIMILAR

Similar colours are directly next to, or near each other on the colour wheel. When used together, these colours can create a soothing effect rather than a harsh intense one. Materials of similar colours such as orange-toned corten steel with red brick or a dark wood, can help to produce a garden that looks well considered and coherent.

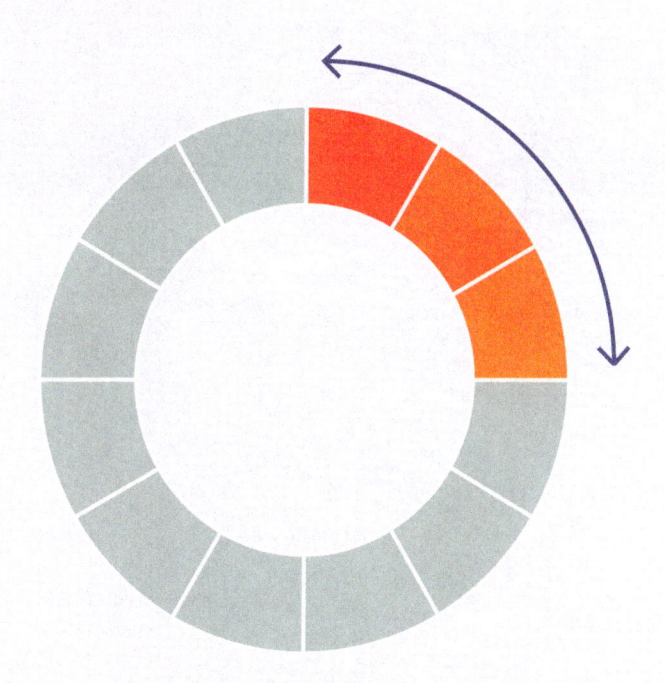

COOL

If you want to create a cool and tranquil garden space, greys and blues are a great way to achieve this. If you choose a cool theme, it's important to actively avoid warm colours as this can create an aggressive accent. Within hardscaping, light-grey coloured gravels and slabs work well as a neutral base.

Planting can be added to introduce further colour and enhance the cool tones - using silver, white and blue plants would be a great addition. Water features or ponds are another way to boost the cool nature of a space.

PASTEL

Pastel colours make for a soft and calming environment whilst still providing some seasonal beauty.

Pastels can be introduced through plants really easily and their delicate hues work well with grasses. Pink, lilac and blue plants are best for complementing smooth sandy toned grasses.

Be careful with yellows - although it is often seen as a pastel colour, some brighter yellows can stand out and break the soft colour palette.

MONOCHROME

Within a monochrome garden it is key to pick your palette and stick to it. It is easy to divert away from this by introducing a few differing colours here and there and this can instantly ruin the impact of the garden. Patterns are a fantastic way of highlighting the monochromatic style - through Moroccan tiles or cushions for example. The planting should be kept mostly green to allow the hardscaping colours to pop.

WARM

A warm garden is where you can be really playful with materials, especially in a coastal garden. Source scrap metals, weathered wood and corten steel to bring some character and a warm dimension. Bronze, yellow, orange and red plants are essential to elevate a warm garden - avoid whites and blues.

BOLD

Vibrant colours work beautifully to create a playful, bold and exciting garden. When designing a bold space, utilise contrasting colours such as blue and orange or purple and yellow. Try to avoid whites and silvers. In a bold garden, solid block colours are a key feature. Painting a wall one block colour and then introducing contrasting colours through planting is a great way to ensure the garden is vibrant and lively.

SUBTLE

A subtle garden lends itself to natural materials and tones. Choosing your textures carefully is vital for consistent subtlety - you wouldn't want to introduce too many rough or sharp materials here. Soft and smooth features are key to creating a garden that's gentle on the eye. Driftwood and shingle work well in subtle gardens because they enhance the natural feel. The beauty of a subtle garden is that you can choose a planting scheme that is either cool or pastel, but it is essential to stick to one scheme or another to ensure the plants balance and complement each other.

128

129

A light coloured backdrop draws the eye to the colour in front.

A pop of colour works really well and the dramatic Acer trees do this so well.

Orange pops stand out and keep good balance.

Why not paint a bench, bringing colour into garden accessories is great way to link areas together.

The pink plants tie in and link with the beach hut shed.

Exciting use of vibrant colour on a simple shed.

TEXTURE SHAPE AND FORM

08

Texture, shape and form can bring gentleness, vibrancy, curiosity, structure and interest to a garden design and although these things are usually thought about on some level, it really is worth your while considering what different types of textures, shapes and form can bring to your space.

Perhaps you want a natural feel with movement and gentleness. Maybe you would like a bright, bold, sharp design. Perhaps you enjoy the formal look of trained trees and straight edges or maybe the informal, wispy style of lavender and grasses flowing freely over path edges.

Thinking through what you really want to project in your garden and choosing materials which reflect your thoughts is absolutely vital to ensure your garden ends up looking as you initially imagined it to.

The following pages will take you through some ideas and hopefully help you to really visualise the end result.

TEXTURE

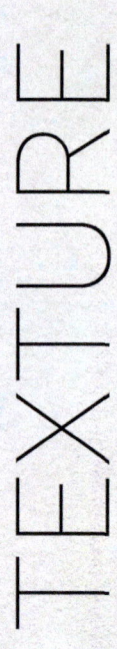

Texture can be introduced to a garden through materials, features and plant choices. When designing and planning, you want to consider the look of all the surface elements to ensure they work together when combined in one space to give the right atmosphere to your design.

Balance and consistency is key to creating a well designed garden, so we would suggest limiting your hard landscaping to three materials and using them to create a visual connection and flow throughout the space.

Different plants can be used in different ways to harness the play of light and shadow and their placing needs to be considered to get the best effect from where they are viewed. Too much of one texture can be inharmonious to the eye unless used in a way to create a dramatic effect, maybe for a small zone. Choosing a mixture of textures with the correct positioning can really help to highlight them all and avoid one from dominating the garden and being overpowering.

It is suggested that a good balance of plant textures is one third fine and two thirds coarse and bold.

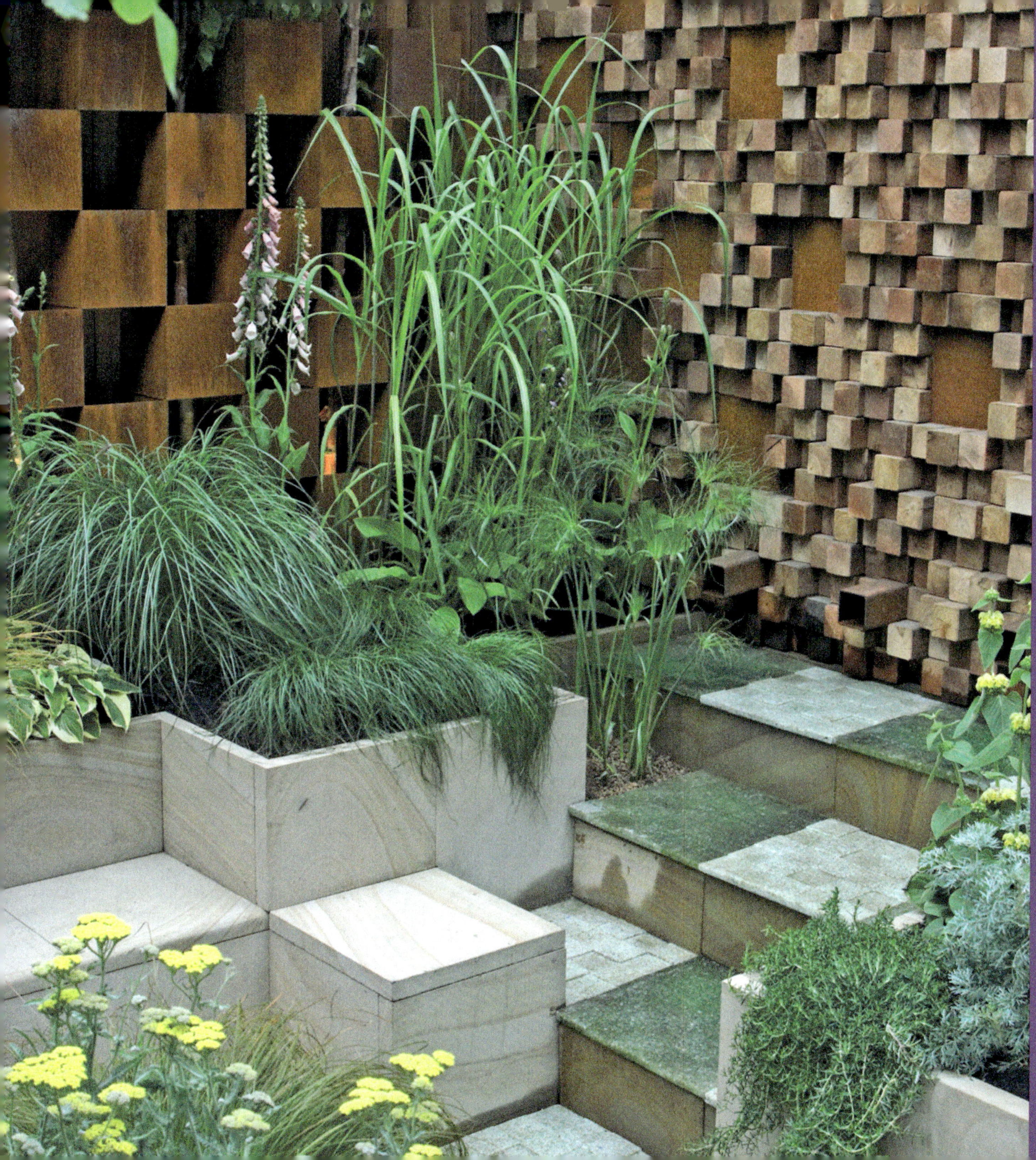

Architectural spiky plants such as *Eryngium* give all year round texture. Their presence within a garden is striking, harsh and reminiscent of a coastal area.

SPIKY

RUSTY

Flaking rust provides rough edges and irregularity and is forever evolving. Scrap metals and groynes are great features to use to introduce this texture.

UNEVEN

Uneven surfaces such as stone cladding or dry stone walls can help to introduce depth, dimension, interest and a feeling of rustic roughness.

The sharp textures of *Agave* and *Phormium* really stand out in planting beds and are excellent used as a natural structural element.

SHARP

GRAIN

Weathered wood and composite decking have unique grainy surfaces providing a rough and bumpy texture which adds a certain rawness to a space.

ROCKY

Gravel is a great substance to use to add more coastal texture to a hard landscaped area and the sound when walking across it adds more interest.

Smooth metals can be used as planters or sculptures to add a seamless and clean texture to your garden and are very often chosen for modern designs.

SEAMLESS

WISPY

Wispy textured plants such as pony tails (*Stipa Tenuissima*) that flutter in the wind help to soften planting beds and introduce a calmness.

FLAT

Flat surfaces such as compressed gravel or porcelain paving provide smoothness and complement a quiet and calming environment.

The calm nature of water can enhance a tranquil space. Water adds interest, especially noticed when moving through or across a solid surface.

WATER

DELICATE

Delicate features such as ornamental grasses have soft tones and bring movement and a certain natural lightness to a space.

Feathered grasses such as fountain grasses (*Pennisetum*) introduce a fluttery gentleness to a planting bed, giving a sense of motion and delicate texture.

FEATHERED

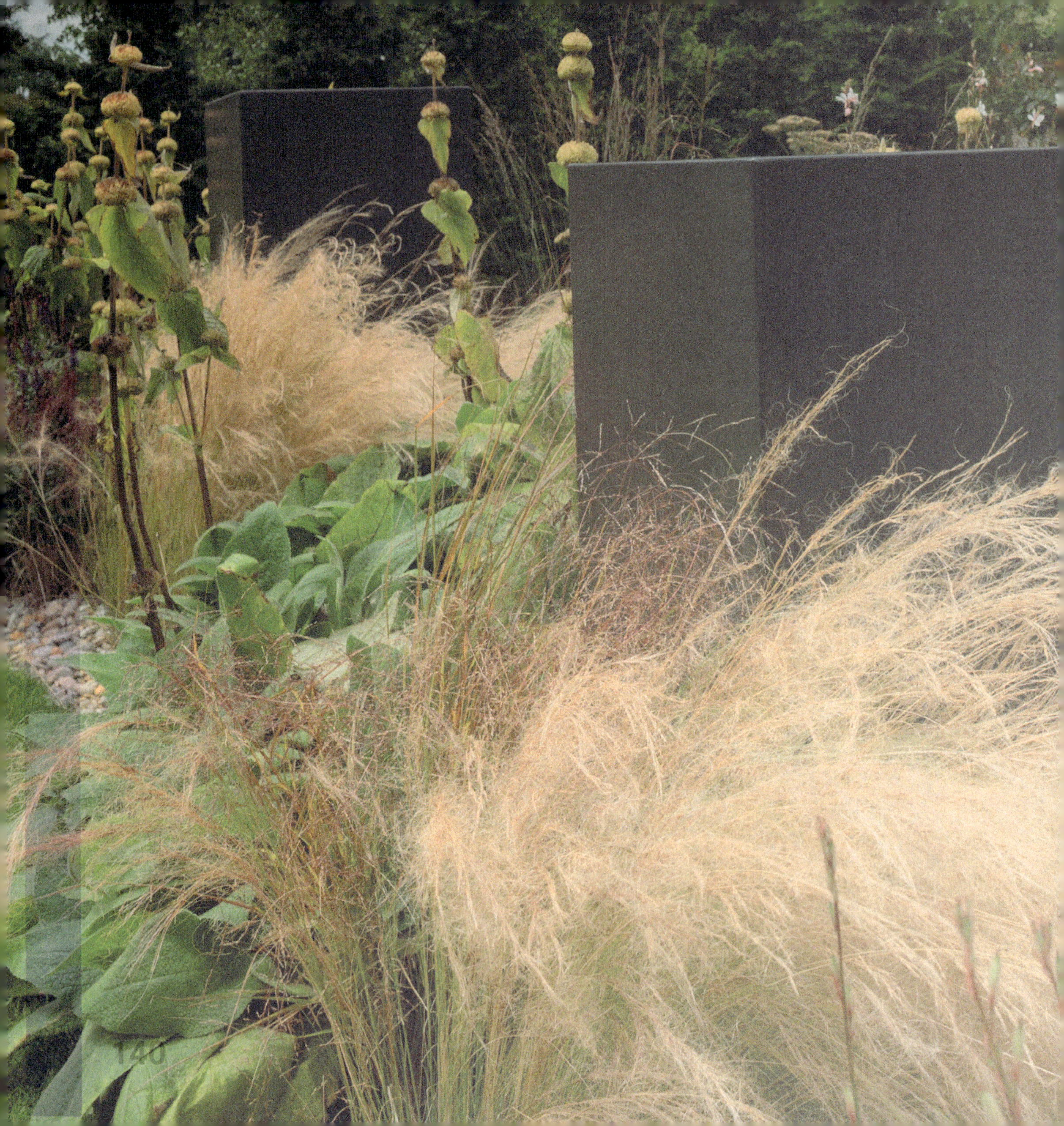

Stipa tenuissima has a delicate and wispy appearance that perfectly complements the coastal theme. It's graceful, swaying fronds evoke the image of grasses found along sandy dunes and coastal cliffs. Wispy textures create a sense of visual lightness in the garden.

SHAPE

The shape of your garden will ultimately form the layout and it is wise to consider your existing landscape when working out which shape to use, although this can be changed.

Informal style gardens tend to have more curved lines and irregular shapes. If your garden boundary already has existing curves, or elements such as a round pond are already present within the space, an informal landscape tends to work best.

Formal gardens are structured, rigid and usually based around straight lines, so naturally these spaces lend themselves to straight-edged shapes. If your garden already hosts straight lines, such as angular fences, square sheds or straight walls, it works well to continue this throughout the design to complement the existing features.

It is important to consider how you are going to navigate through your space - a well-thought-out journey can totally transform the experience. The journey can involve focal points and features which all have an impact on how the garden is shaped.

Form (three-dimensional objects) adds interest and should enhance the experience, flowing and blending within the overall shape. The following pages look at this in more detail.

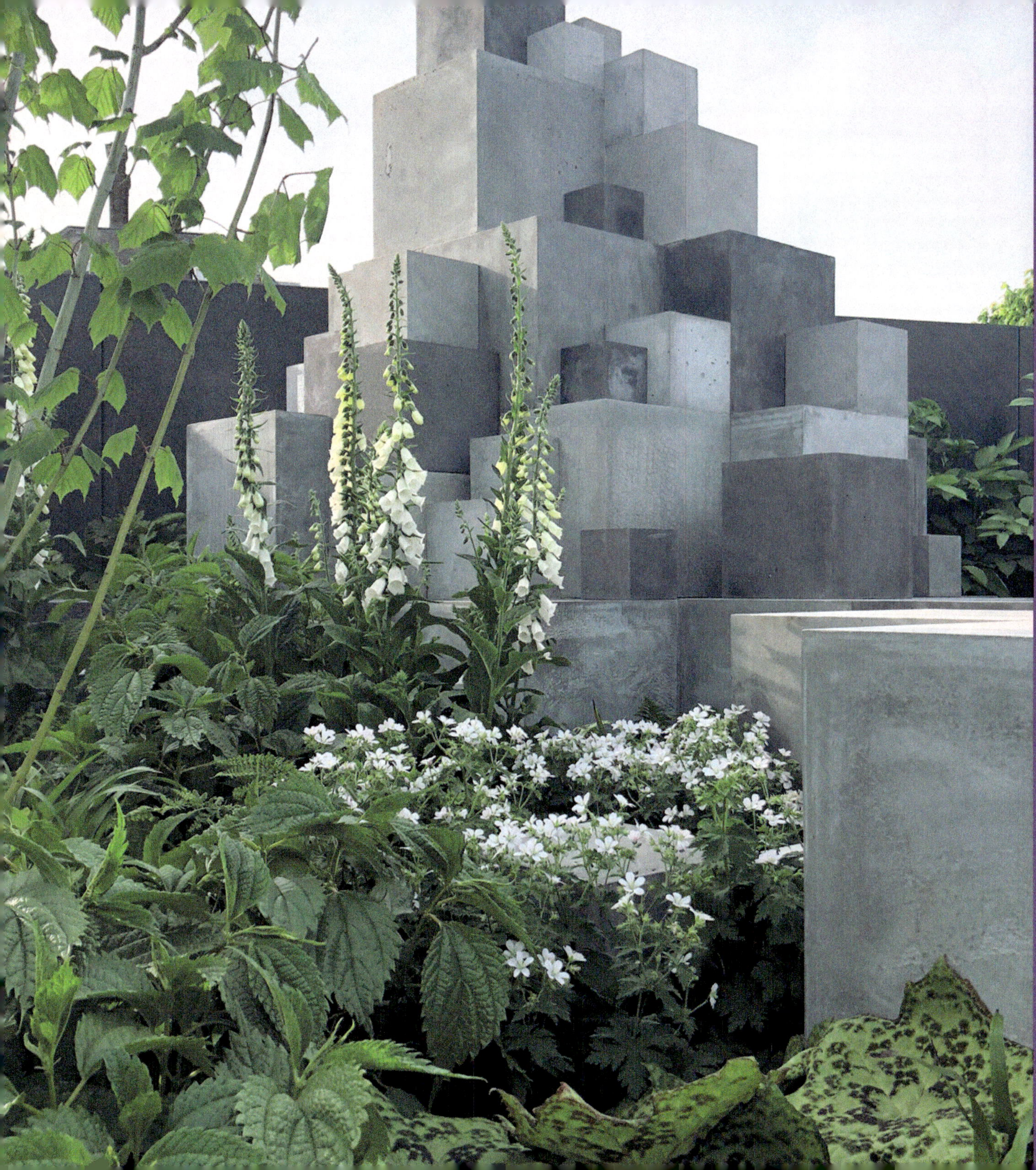

CURVES AND LINES

Using curves within a garden is a great way to introduce a natural free-flowing space. If you want your garden to offer an adventurous and meandering journey, curves are a useful tool to achieve this.

Straight lines work best when they compliment the architecture of your house - you can line up paths in the garden to doors and windows on the house, and align square planters to wall edges - the options are endless. Straight lines are great for those who love symmetry and crispness.

Positioning a curved bench alongside the sinuous water rill and circular lawn creates a smooth transition that doesn't disrupt the flow or visual allure of the organic landscape. The bench's winding contour complements the meandering course of the water feature.

PLANTING FORM

ROUNDED

Some plants naturally form into round shapes whilst others would need to be pruned regularly to keep the neat rounded effect.

ARCHED

Branches tend to fan out from the top. They are good for a more informal garden. *Buddleja davidii* 'Grand Cascade' is a lovely example.

DOMED

A dome shaped plant, such as *Hydrangea paniculata* 'Limelight' can happily sit within a formal or informal garden.

COLUMNAR

With a tall, slim form, columnar plants can be focal points, bring height to a space and are often used to disguise or break up walls or fences.

SPIKY

A spiky plant can give more of an informal feel. They are good to have in a natural coastal garden and give year-round interest.

TRAINED

These are ideal for a formal garden, giving a sense of order and they can be trained into a variety of different shapes.

FEATURE FORM

Introducing a 3d feature to the garden can really enhance the landscape. This could be something as simple as a mirror or a small water feature or as complex and extravagant as a large sculpture.

Features can be contemporary or traditional. They make ideal focal points, drawing the eye to a certain area and are a great way of adding further height or dimension to a space.

The size of the feature is really important to consider - if your garden is small, you would not choose to have an imposing sculpture, and if you have a larger garden, a small mirror would be lost.

You might want to use a number of sculptures of the same form to create a dramatic look. For example, placing several different sized cubes in and around the garden can be an effective use of form.

You might want to choose a feature that will lead your eye up the garden such as a sculpture at the end of a path or a water rill. Archways can draw your eye and spark curiosity to explore a new area of the garden.

You might want to consider mirroring the planting with a similar shaped feature - small metal spheres placed amongst buxus balls can bring a sense of unity to a space.

The use of varying-sized cubes within the sculpture introduces a dynamic visual contrast, creating an interesting interplay of proportions and scales. These themes can be reflected in other elements such as the planting and ground levels in order to create a sense of visual cohesion.

The cube is a symmetrical and balanced geometric shape. When it is placed on a square paving slab, which is also a symmetrical shape, it creates a harmonious and visually pleasing composition. It also subtly plays on the relationship between the 3D and 2D form.

JOURNEY

Many people think you need a large garden to create a garden journey, but with thought given to the space and the layout, small gardens can take you on a wonderful journey full of interest. Plants are a good way to direct you around the garden and lead the eye.

You can screen areas to create rooms or send yourself around paths with interesting features or focal points along the way.

Coastal gardens lend themselves to shingle paths which is a very natural solution to the journey of the garden. Curved paths work well for creating a meandering journey and can be complemented with points of interest such as benches or sculptures, which create a visual break.

PATTERNS

Patterns can be used to create wonderful structure in the garden. They can be created by the lines on fences, repeated archways or clay paver pathways. They can also be formed by repeating objects, such as sculptures, or manipulating plants, such as training a climber into a diamond shape.

Circular, straight or irregular patterned tiles add dynamism to a formal garden. For a more informal look, you could choose mosaic tiles.

Perforated corten steel or aluminium panels are a great way to bring pattern into the garden, or for a more temporary feature, you could simply add a patterned rug and cushions to a seating area.

This corten steel panel is perforated with a foliage pattern. This mimics the planting and filters the light creating patterns on surrounding surfaces, adding another element of interest.

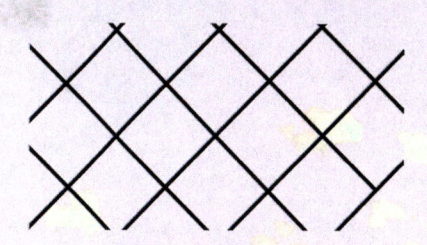

This design subtly connects the small squares within the mosaic tiles with the larger tiles in the main pathway by reflecting the diamond shape. It adds a professional feel as it is clear the layout has been intelligently designed to add extra interest.

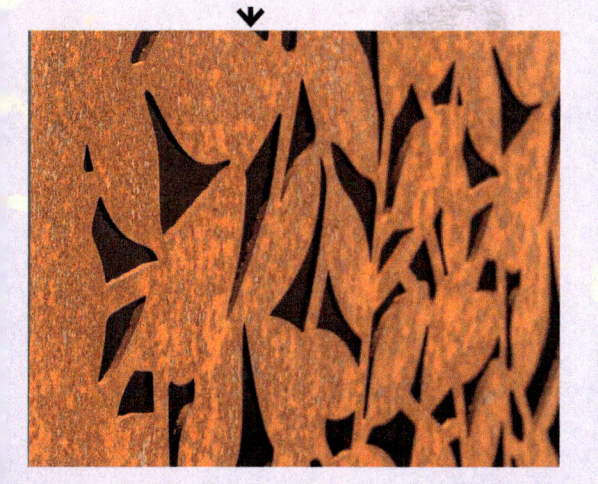

DESIGN PREPARATION

09

Hopefully by this stage of our book you have gained inspiration from lots of different elements which build up a garden and more specifically, a coastal garden.

Coastal garden style is whatever you make of it. Some people may enjoy the idea of including lots of personal items that remind them of the coast, others may want to recreate their favourite coastal areas. There is so much creativity you can put into designing a coastal garden - personalising them is so much fun.

It's now time to design your very own coastal garden - the following section will give you all the information you need to draw out your plans, choose the perfect plants and work out your build budget.

This section should give you your masterplan to enable you to complete the project. It is of course very important to check with your local authority regarding any conditions which may limit build and design works in your garden. Maybe you live in a conservation area, a listed building or perhaps tree preservation orders are in place. Some elements of your build may need permissions, so make sure you have all this in place before starting so that you can fully focus on your project worry-free.

RESEARCH

This book is just the starting point - there is a lot to consider when you're making decisions about what you want and what is possible for your garden. Research can give you visual inspiration, the chance to think through the ultimate function and layout of your garden and how to build it within your budget.

Inspiration can come from many places - sometimes it arrives completely unexpectedly. If you want to go and find it, you could take a walk along the beach - maybe pack a sketchbook with you to make notes and doodles and try to piece together aspects and features that work. Take photos of things that you like but can't identify (plants for instance), so that you can find out once you're back home. Maybe take some time to visit public gardens to see how they are laid out, how they flow and how walking through them makes you feel and ask yourself why that might be.

If your garden is not on level ground, you may need to hire a landscape architect to survey it and let you know exactly what is and isn't possible regarding moving earth and creating levels.

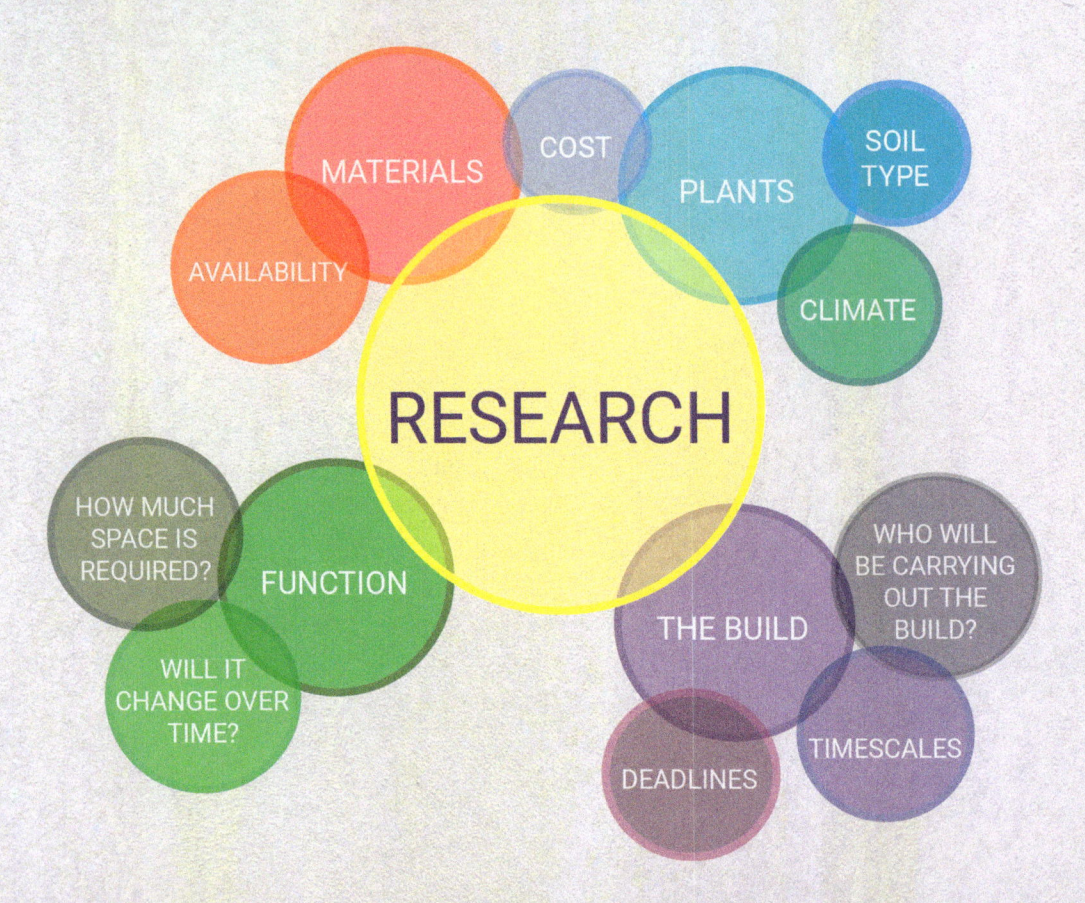

RESEARCH

- MATERIALS
- COST
- PLANTS
- SOIL TYPE
- AVAILABILITY
- CLIMATE
- HOW MUCH SPACE IS REQUIRED?
- FUNCTION
- WILL IT CHANGE OVER TIME?
- THE BUILD
- WHO WILL BE CARRYING OUT THE BUILD?
- DEADLINES
- TIMESCALES

BUDGET

45% **25%** **10%** **10%** **10%**

Example guide of cost percentages

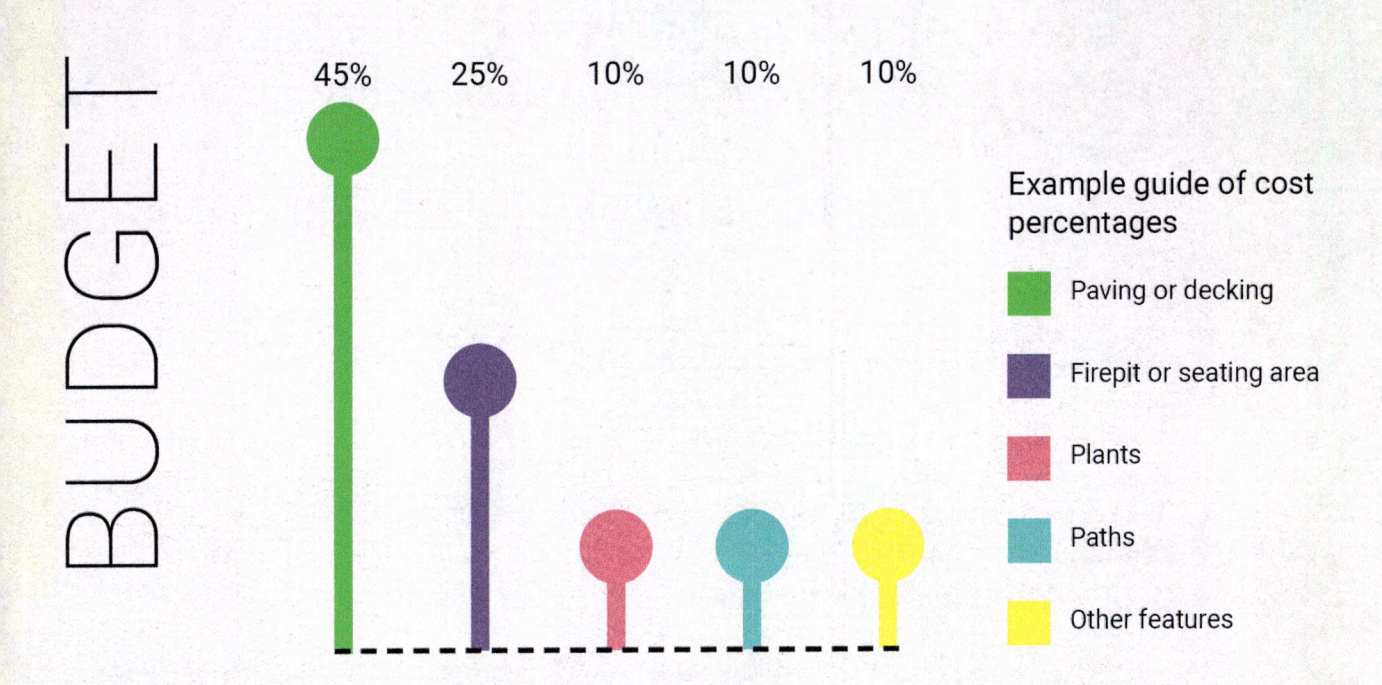

- Paving or decking
- Firepit or seating area
- Plants
- Paths
- Other features

This is quite possibly the most important element of designing your new garden. It is easy to design a spectacular garden, but without research into build costs it can be a fruitless exercise. The easiest way to do this is to break down all the main elements you are looking for, such as a patio, firepit, plants, paths etc. It would be a good idea to look online for a guide of costs. Most people will have a budget in mind, but always remember that a beautifully designed garden is a worthy investment and can substantially add value to your property, as well as be a wonderful space for you to enjoy.

We have given a very loose guide of how much each main element can take out of your budget above. As a general rule, the hard landscaping, such as patios, costs the most money, although we always say do not underestimate the planting cost, allowing around 10% for this, as plants are usually the element that brings the garden together.

It's important to do your research to get this right for the garden you want to create and enjoy.

CONCEPT MOOD BOARD

A mood board is a collection of images that, together, show a good representation of how you see your future garden. It should include anything that you've drawn inspiration from.

When collating a mood board think about the smaller details as well as the overall concept and theme. A mood board can contain close-up images displaying texture or patterns as well as planting colours and materials. It can show whole areas such as a firepit space or dining area.

The key to the mood board is being able to create a concept that you can glance at and instantly gain an understanding of the garden design intention, and the final effect you wish to achieve. Of course, these are just inspiring ideas - your garden will be a unique compilation of influences.

Anything goes - cut-outs from magazines, photographs, drawings, colour swatches. You might choose to digitally create a mood board on specialised websites and apps.

Seeing the ideas come together can help you visualise your dream garden. Having it accessible - out on your desk, pinned to a board or clipped on string on your wall, would be a great way to keep the inspiration flowing!

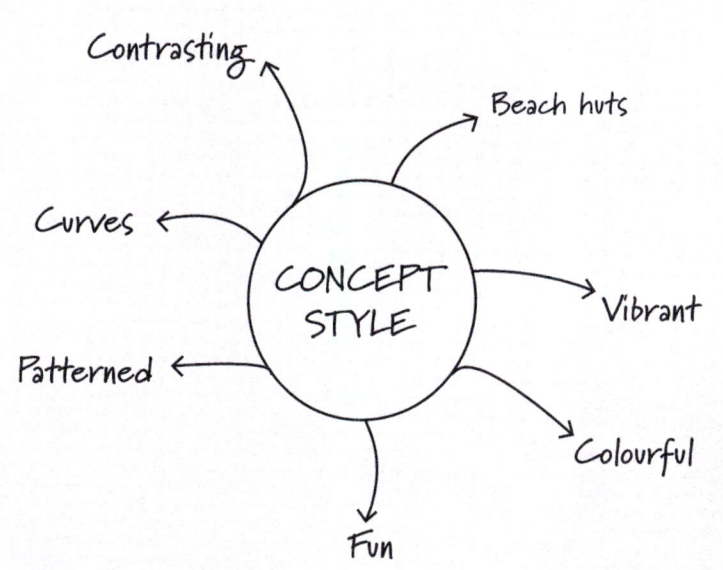

CONCEPT STYLE

- Contrasting
- Curves
- Patterned
- Beach huts
- Vibrant
- Colourful
- Fun

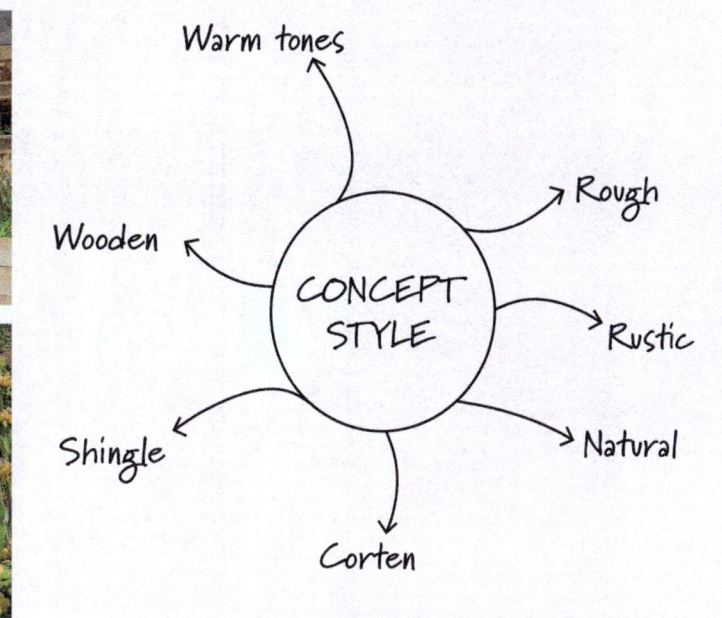

CONCEPT STYLE

- Warm tones
- Rough
- Rustic
- Natural
- Corten
- Shingle
- Wooden

157

COMPLETION

INSPIRATION

159

COMPLETION

INSPIRATION

161

MEASURE AND DRAW

10

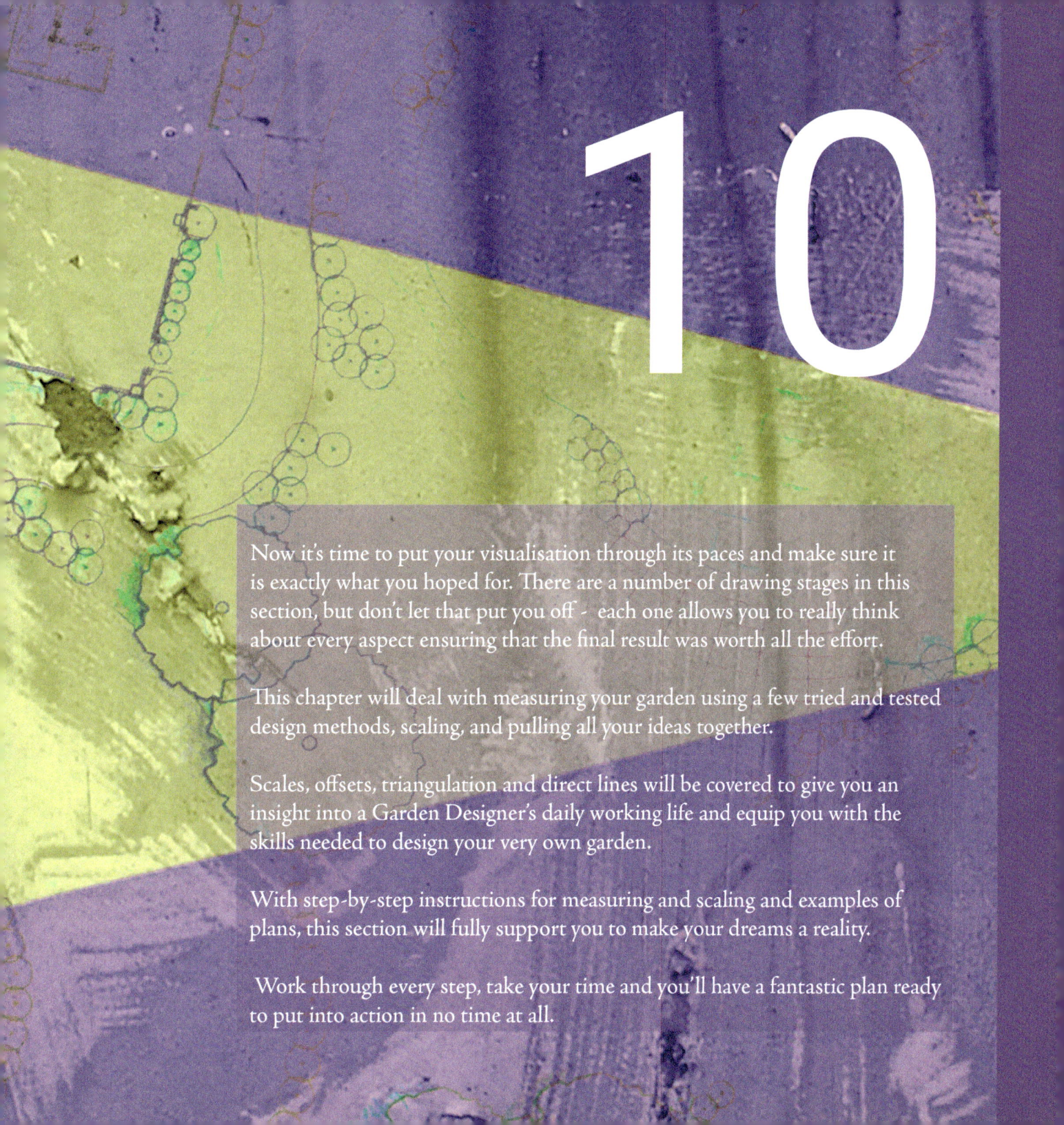

Now it's time to put your visualisation through its paces and make sure it is exactly what you hoped for. There are a number of drawing stages in this section, but don't let that put you off - each one allows you to really think about every aspect ensuring that the final result was worth all the effort.

This chapter will deal with measuring your garden using a few tried and tested design methods, scaling, and pulling all your ideas together.

Scales, offsets, triangulation and direct lines will be covered to give you an insight into a Garden Designer's daily working life and equip you with the skills needed to design your very own garden.

With step-by-step instructions for measuring and scaling and examples of plans, this section will fully support you to make your dreams a reality.

Work through every step, take your time and you'll have a fantastic plan ready to put into action in no time at all.

MEASURING

One of the most important stages of designing your own garden is measuring the elements and putting it on paper in the correct scale. You need to make sure your garden is drawn accurately and there are a few different methods you can use to measure your garden including triangulation, direct line measurements and offsets.

Direct line is simply measuring along a straight line and is useful when measuring the length of a straight wall or house wall. If only it was always that easy. From here, you can use triangulation and offsets to accurately measure distances between areas and the shapes of irregular features.

The triangulation method creates lots of triangular shape measurements from a fixed point (on your house), which allows you to accurately measure major landmarks in the garden and the distances between them. Your major landmarks will include the boundary, the house and any existing trees or other features which will form part of your design.

Offsets measurements involve laying a tape through say, a cluster of trees, and measuring the distance from the tape to each tree. This is a useful method in this situation as it is quicker than the triangulation of each tree. It is also useful for curved paths and flower beds.

If you use all these simple methods as and when necessary, you'll have an accurately scaled picture of your garden layout in no time.

DIRECT LINE

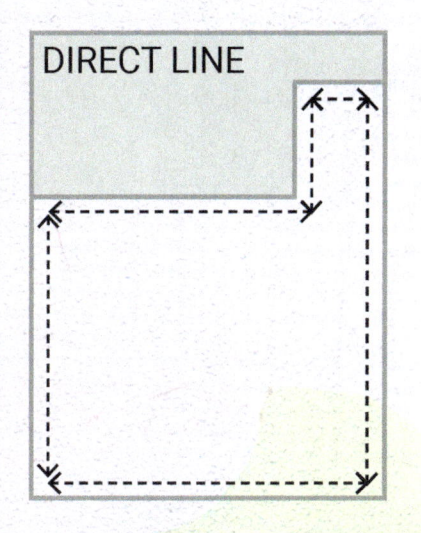

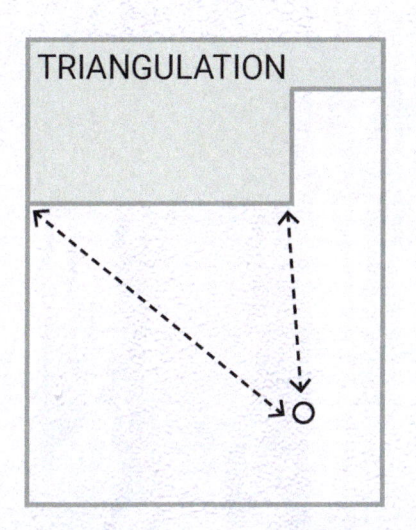

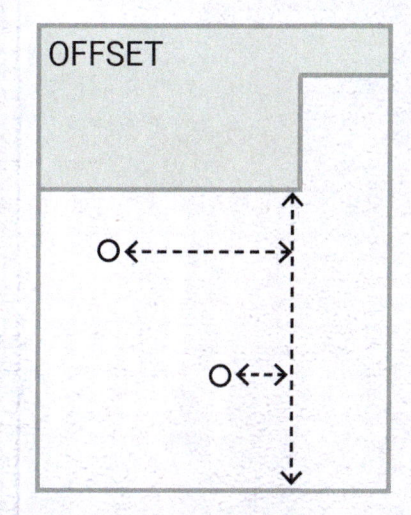

TRIANGULATION

OFFSET

TRIANGULATION METHOD

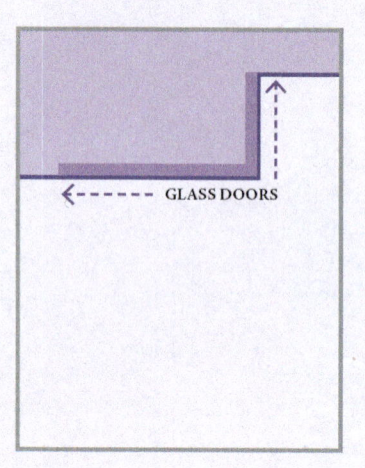

01

← - - - - GLASS DOORS

Measure the house including windows, doors, drains, manhole covers and changes of depth.

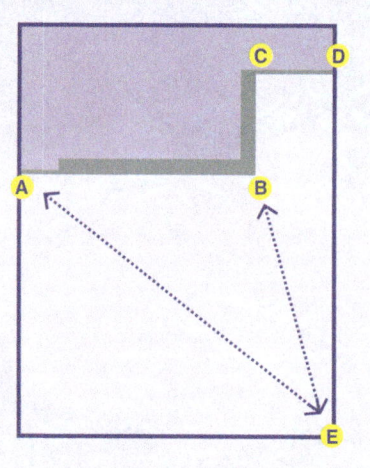

04

From another point on the house (e.g. B) measure to the same point (E) The larger the triangles the better. Your new measurement will be named BE.

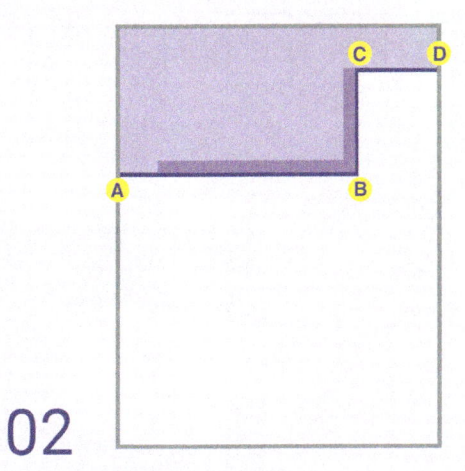

02

Label corner points with letters alphabetically and start with A.

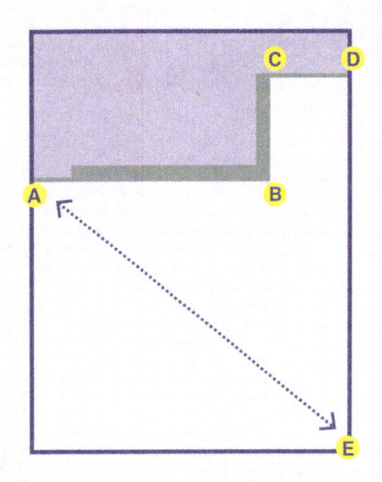

03

Measure the feature or boundary from this point (A). Name the new point (E) and name this measurement accordingly (AE).

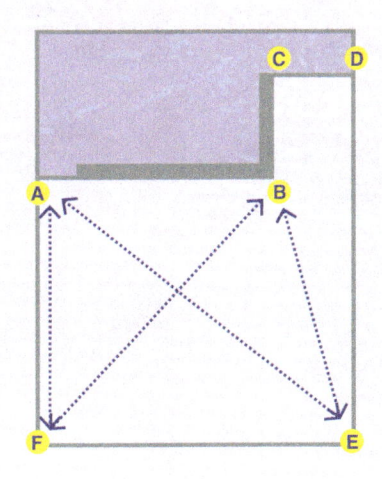

05

Now continue until you have all points accounted for. We recommend using a reel tape longer than the length of your garden for accuracy.

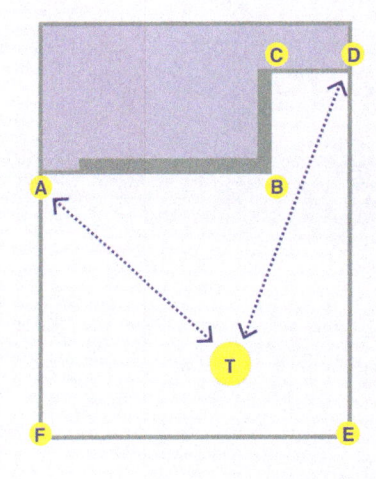

06

Once you have all the boundaries plotted, use the same technique for plotting any features or trees. Measure from the centre middle of the feature from either side.

167

PLOTTING MEASUREMENTS

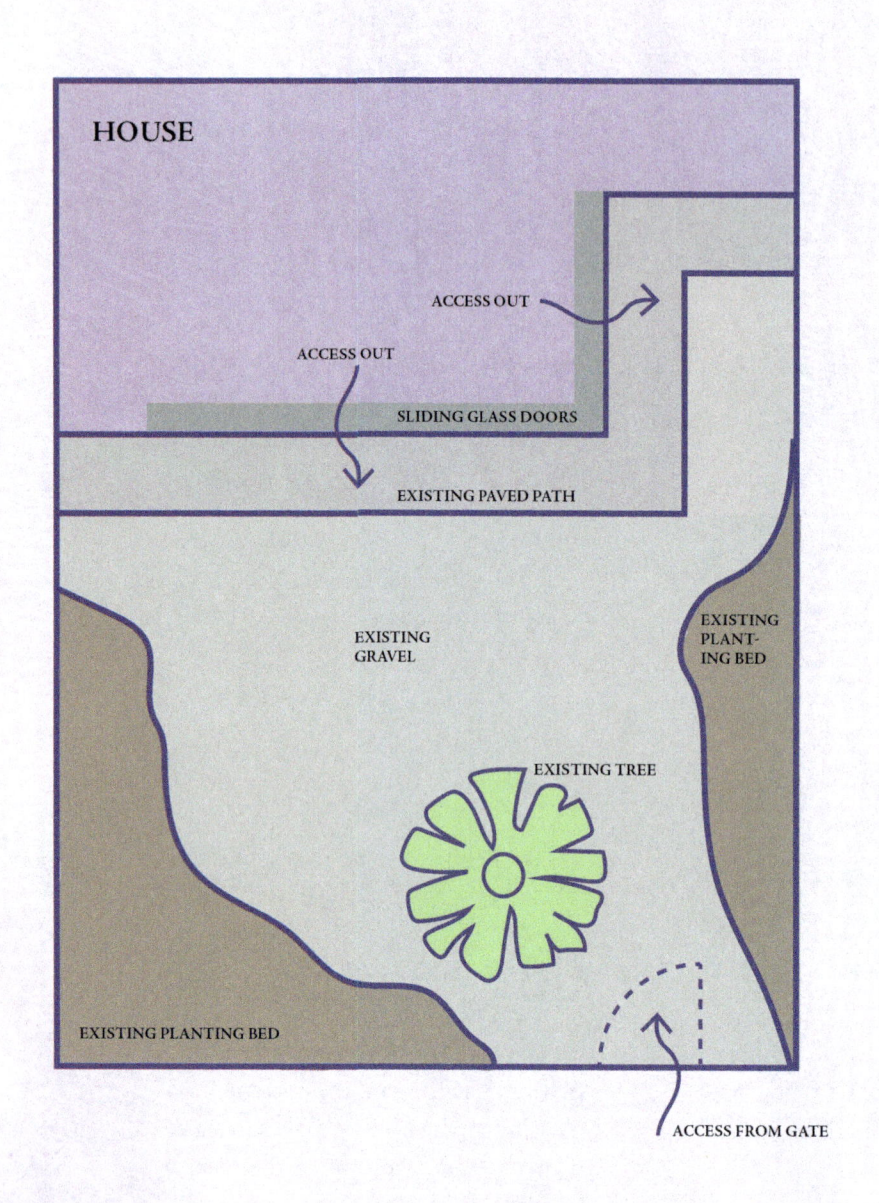

HOUSE

ACCESS OUT

ACCESS OUT

SLIDING GLASS DOORS

EXISTING PAVED PATH

EXISTING GRAVEL

EXISTING PLANTING BED

EXISTING TREE

EXISTING PLANTING BED

ACCESS FROM GATE

HOUSE

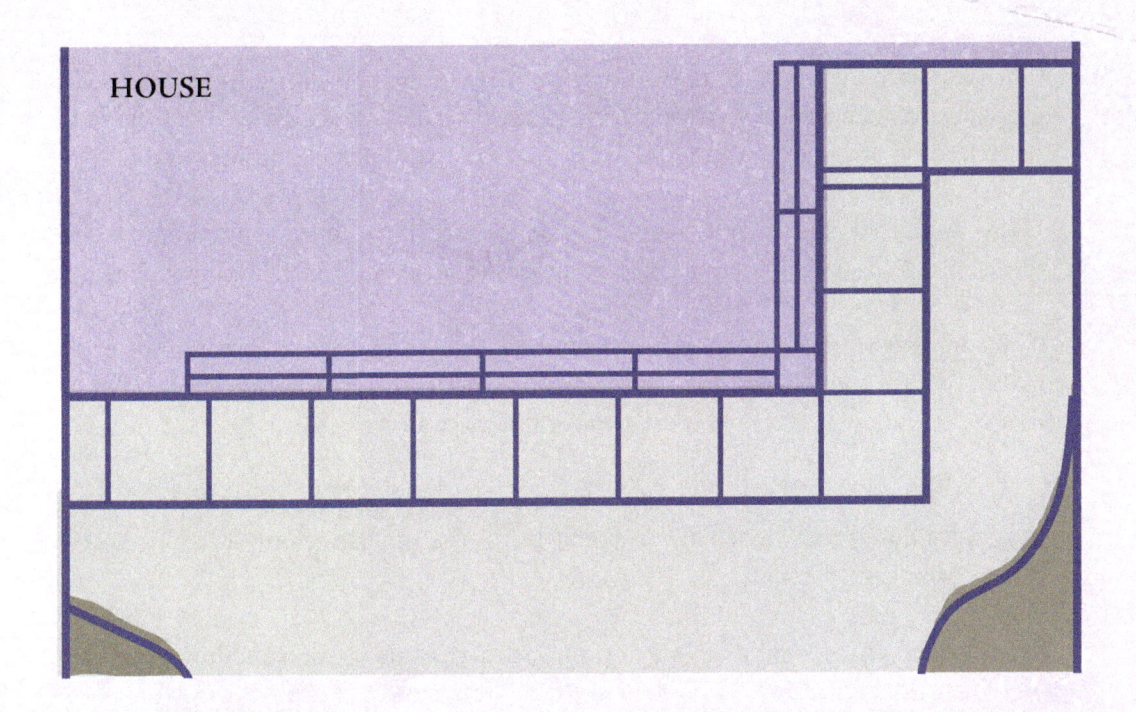

After measuring your garden using the methods stated in the previous pages, you need to turn this information into a visual map on paper (or digitally) that you can use to adapt and lay out the concepts of your garden design. For paper drawn designs, a sharp pencil and a scale ruler are essential pieces of kit. The ruler you use depends on the size of the area you're designing.

As a general rule, for gardens 15m x 15m or less, a 1:50 ruler would suffice. If your area is bigger than this, then a 1:100 scale ruler would be more appropriate. A 1:100 scale ruler implies that for every one metre you measured, this will be shown on the paper as one centimetre.

A3 paper will be fine for plotting small to medium gardens. You could always increase this size to A2 or A1 for larger gardens. Draw the house first and from there plot each of the measurement points you have taken. This can involve a bit of rubbing out dots, but you can always trace over the final layout.

When finished, you will have your blank canvas to work on. Of course you could always use any CAD program of your choice to create the design digitally.

DRAWING YOUR LAYOUT

Once you have a vision in your head from the inspiration you gained from your research and mood board, you need to start your first sketched plan. This plan should only be blocking out where certain areas and features should be placed; it's the skeleton framework.

Use your plotted plan of your current garden to trace the outline of the garden and work within those borders. Remember to use the same measurement scale as the original plotting.

Consider how you plan to use your garden. There should be a natural flow and consistency that makes you feel comfortable and relaxed as you make your way through - an ease of movement that is not punctuated by awkward areas or impracticalities.

Access paths need to be considered for functionality and purpose; imagine how you walk around the garden doing tasks on a daily or weekly basis. You can use coloured arrows to represent this if it helps your visualisation.

Think about what it would be like to sit in each area of the garden and how you get from A to B. You will be the one using the garden, so think about how you want to use your space and which areas need easy access. Also consider privacy and sun direction and movement at this point - will you need to add some trees for privacy or will you use screening or overhead cover?

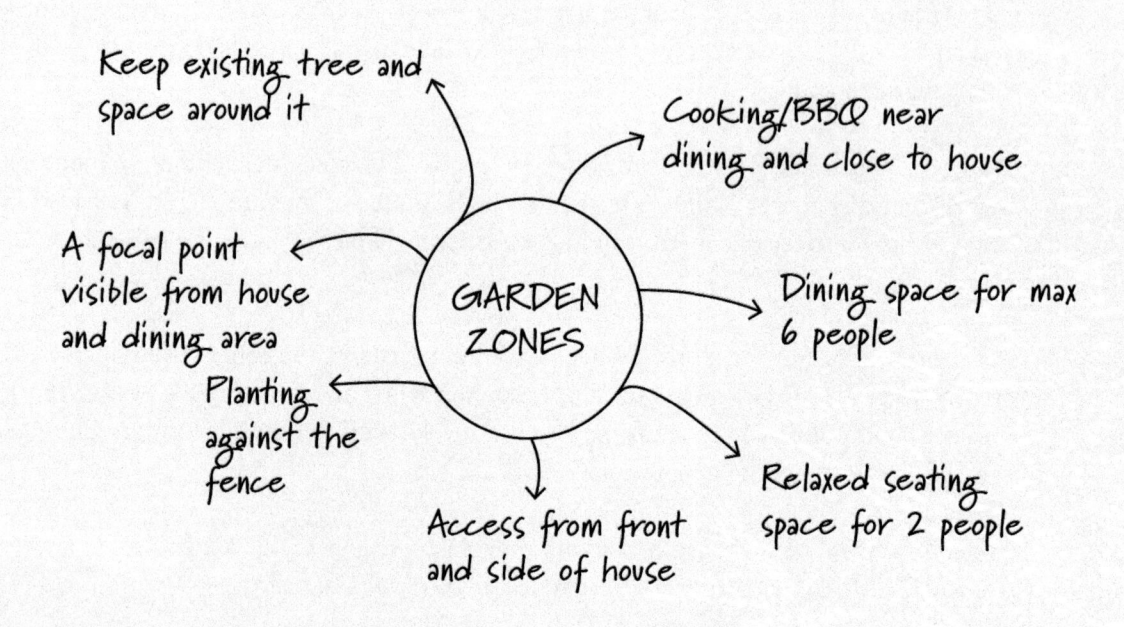

GARDEN ZONES

- Keep existing tree and space around it
- Cooking/BBQ near dining and close to house
- A focal point visible from house and dining area
- Dining space for max 6 people
- Planting against the fence
- Access from front and side of house
- Relaxed seating space for 2 people

BBQ

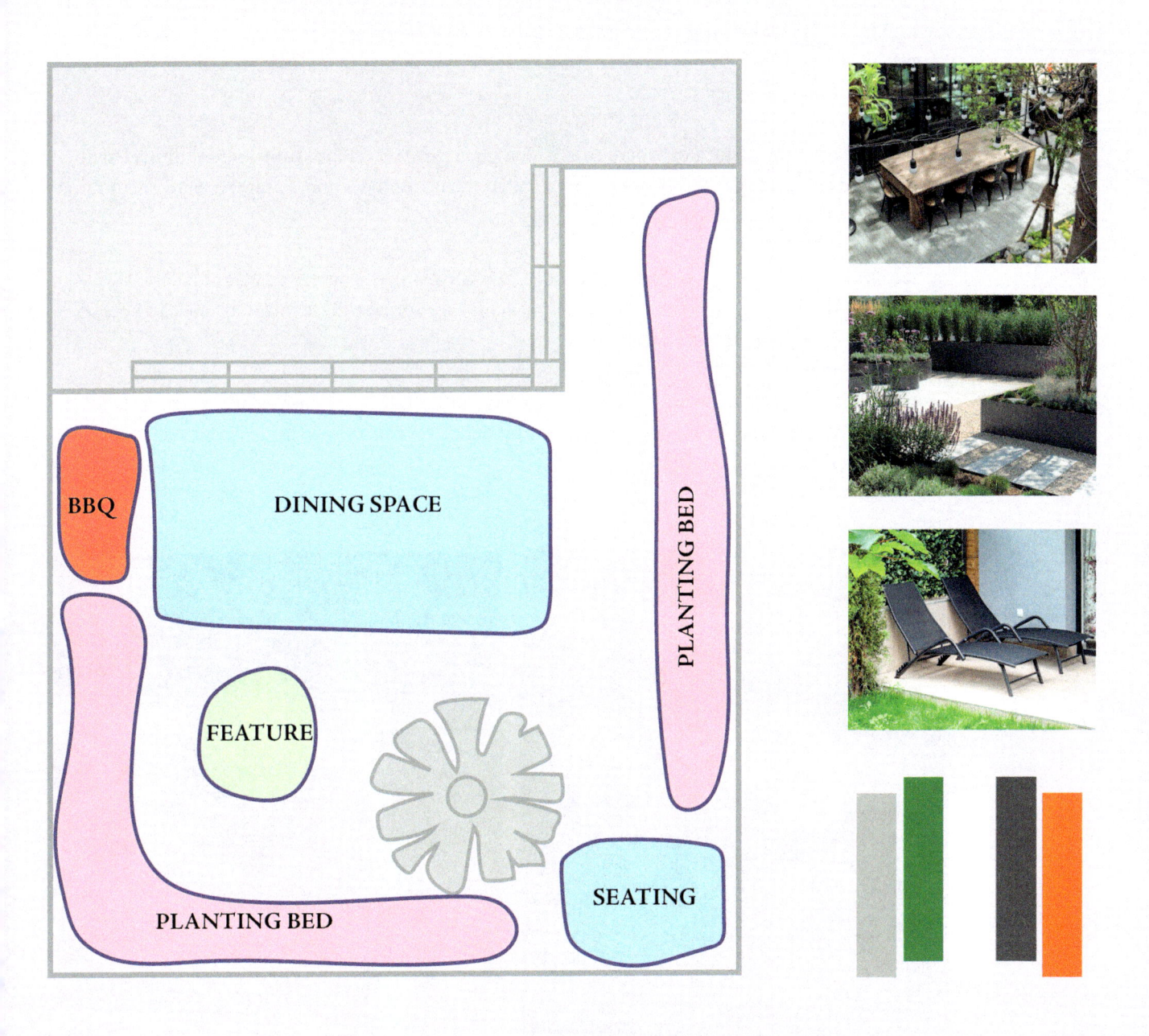

DINING SPACE

PLANTING BED

FEATURE

SEATING

PLANTING BED

171

ADDING DETAIL

Remember the importance of decisions regarding curved lines vs. straight lines and whether you are looking to create an informal or formal space when designing your plan. How and where will your coastal elements fit into your design? Consider viewpoints from key areas of the garden and how they connect to other aspects.

Once you have a rough idea of where things will go, it's time to create your second draft. Part of the purpose of this stage is to confirm some rough measurements and sizing, so as to ensure that you are drawing it at the right scale.

When creating this sketch you want to ensure that the features you are using are balanced throughout the garden, so if there are multiple sculptures or coastal features, be sure to spread them out evenly - usually odd numbers are best.

Once you have a scaled drawing of your design, it's time to add annotations to clearly state what materials and features you are going to use and where. You can even include images of these next to your notes for clear indication.

GRAVEL PATH

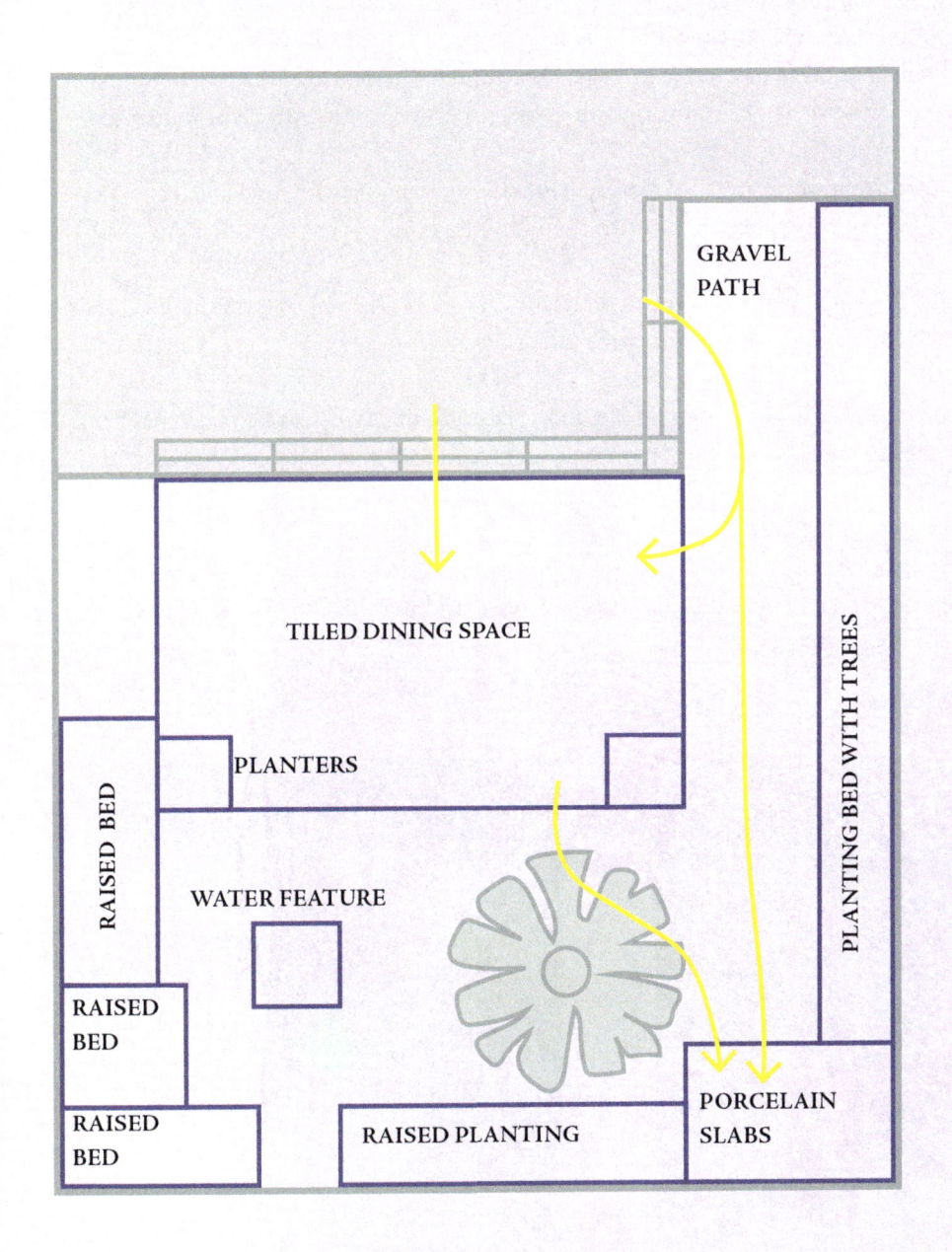

TILED DINING SPACE

PLANTERS

PLANTING BED WITH TREES

RAISED BED

WATER FEATURE

RAISED BED

RAISED BED

RAISED PLANTING

PORCELAIN SLABS

This stage doesn't have to be fully detailed, but searching for some images may help you advance to the next level.

173

FINALISING DESIGN

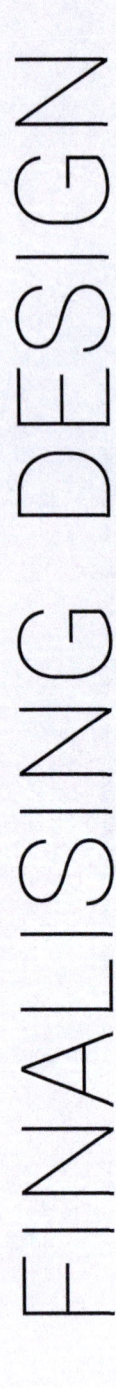

Now you have thought about the size of each area, make this even more specific by fully researching the materials you want to use and the standard sizes they are available in. This can help influence and finalise the size of each area. If you would like the seating area to be comprised of whole uniform slabs, draw the size accordingly to avoid small cuts and wastage of materials.

This sketch will be used when ordering any materials, such as paving or shingle, as well as when building your garden, whether by yourself or with the help of a landscaper.

If you want to include any large features such as sculptures or even trees, allow the space for this and if you have sourced specific items draw in their exact dimensions.

Think about the final look of the garden and if the materials will marry up and complement one another - you want to avoid using too many materials and making the garden look messy and unconsidered.

You can add detailed annotations if required to help during construction. This is a good time to annotate where existing structures are such as taps, drains and manhole covers as well as the heights of design features such as raised beds.

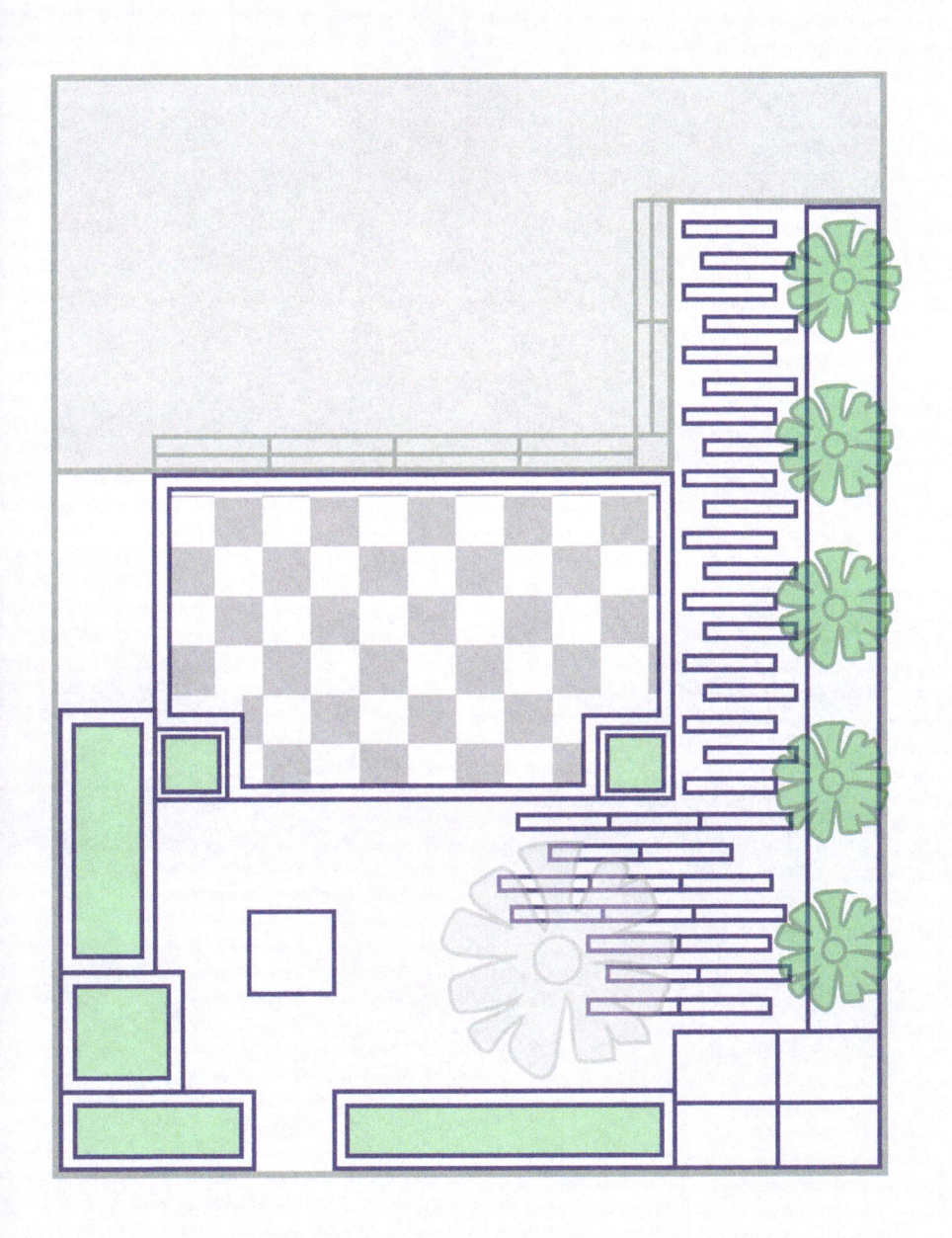

Now your design is finalised, you can help to convey your ideas with some more specific mood board images. Think about the exact materials you want to use, their colour and texture and how they will work together.

175

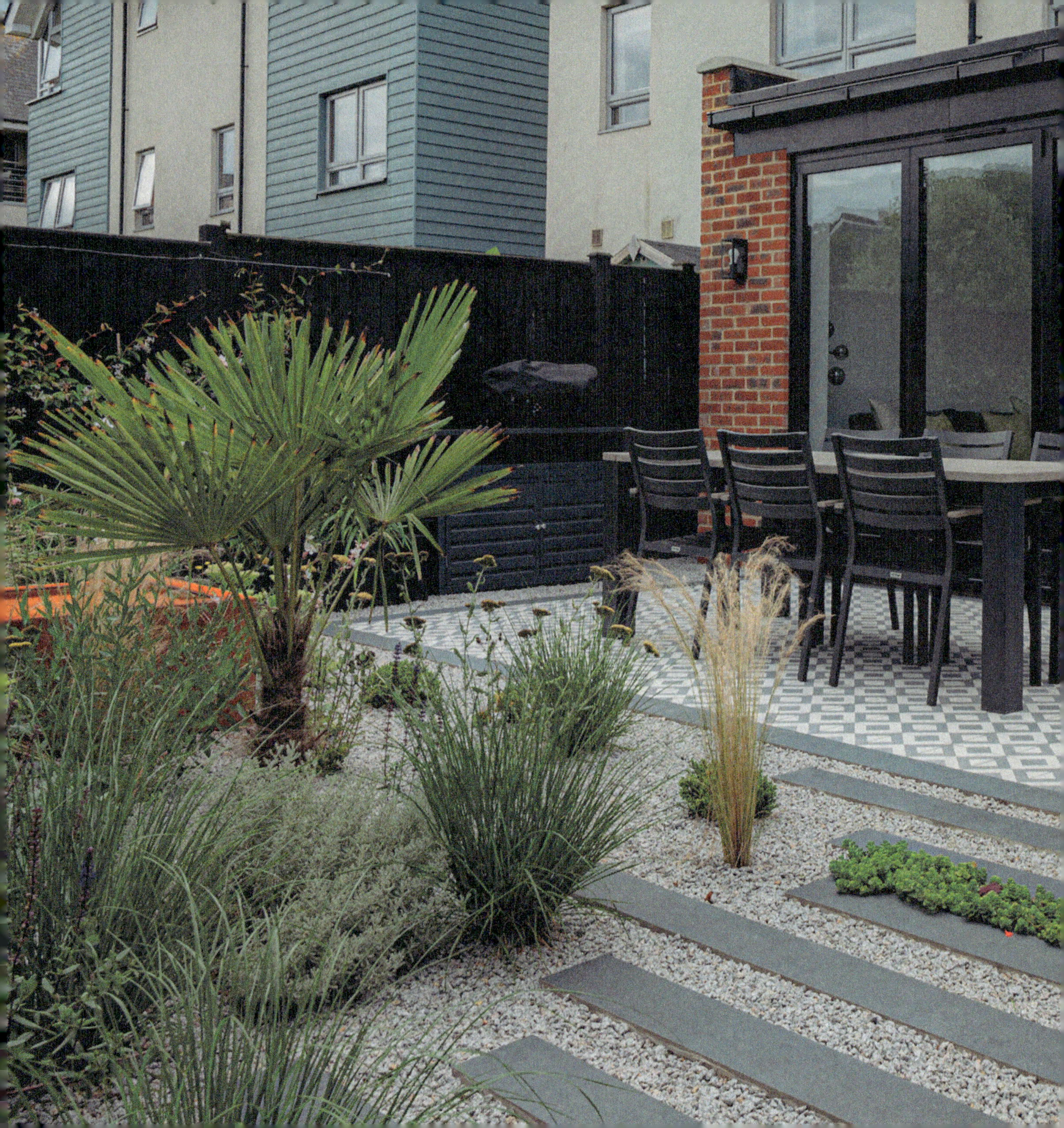

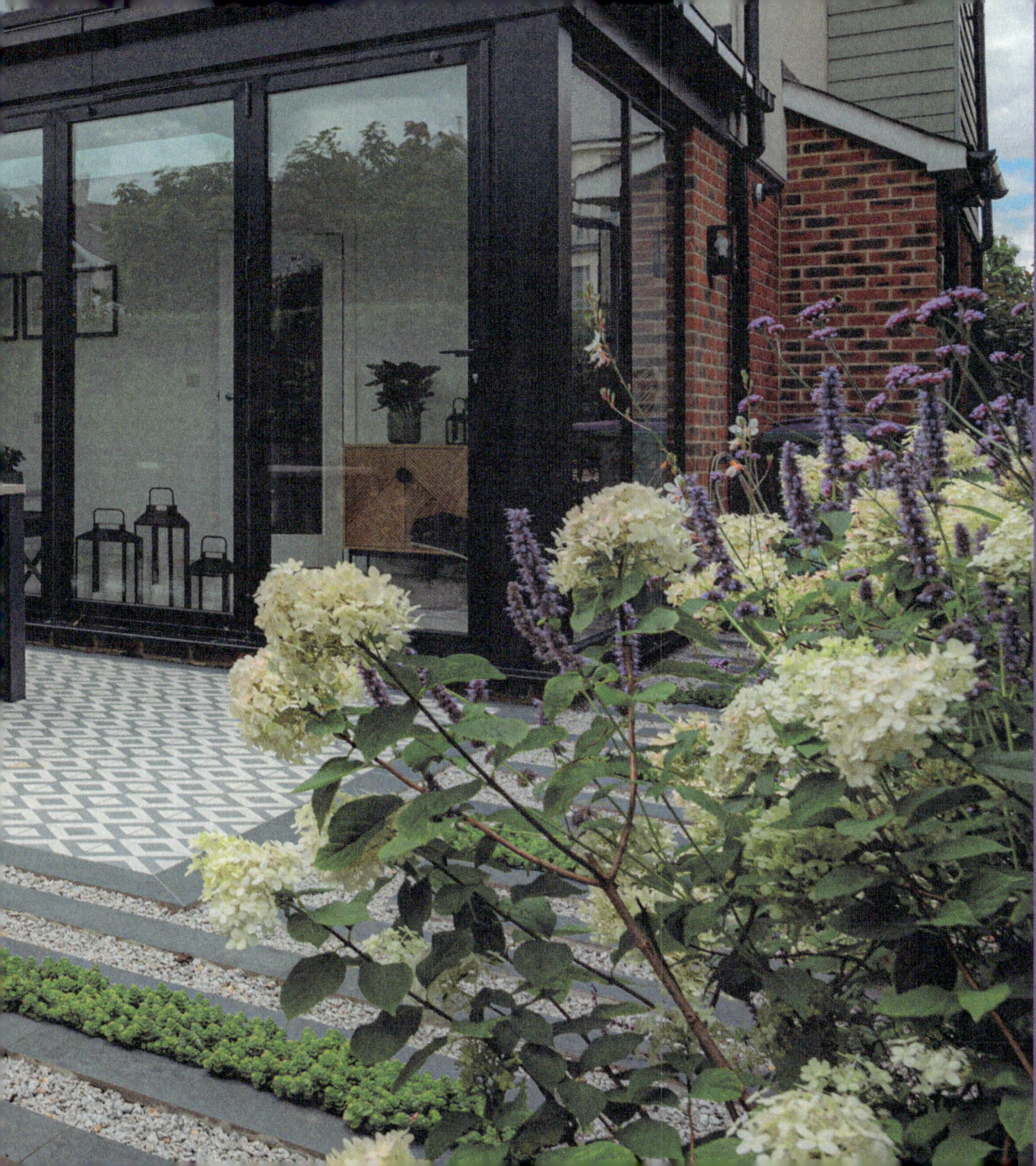

PLANTS AND PLANTING

11

Coastal flora has adapted to survive harsh weather conditions – hardy plants that are accustomed to surviving in exposed areas with drying winds, drought, blazing sunshine, and salty air. Poor soil can typically be added to the mixture as well. This implies that a variety of these hardy coastal plants are tough and able to cope with whatever your garden provides and this can indeed be a correct assumption to a certain extent.

Some of our most beautiful coastal plants will happily adapt to a garden environment and tend not to need much mollycoddling, although this is not true for all. It really depends on whether you can offer the ideal conditions to give them the best chance to thrive. Most coastal flowers and plants tend to be happier in nutrient-poor soil and some are quite content with just a couple of layers of gravel. They are pretty self-sufficient and tough and can look utterly beautiful in a garden, bringing the coastal feel very naturally.

Plants really do bring a scheme together and need to be considered carefully. It's hard not to just buy everything you like the look of and hope to find a spot when you get home, but in reality, having a much more strict approach can really ensure that your garden looks its best. Once you've decided on the style of planting or the colour scheme that works best in your design, sticking to that will ensure the best result.

COASTAL PLANTS

This section is intended to give you some inspiration and information about plants that work well in a coastal garden design. We have included plants that evoke a coastal atmosphere and are very adaptable to their environment. There are many more plants you may wish to consider that wouldn't fit into this book, but our chosen selection could be used to kit out any garden with an abundance of texture, colour and shape.

We have a useful key to help guide you, which will tell you if a plant is drought resistant, native, its preferred aspect and its flowering times. Spending some time on ensuring your choice gives year-round interest is time well spent.

Many coastal plants are naturally tough and drought resistant and therefore a good option when considering the environment and its needs and changes. It also saves you having to water daily during the summer months.

Native plants have spent many years adapting to the local climate and environmental conditions, so they should be lower maintenance (including less watering from you unless it's a hot summer) and perfectly suitable for our local wildlife.

Protecting and increasing the number of native plants helps to support our environment, so if you can include a good number of native and drought resistant plants, do - your garden will thank you for it and you'll be rewarded with a beautiful display that pretty much looks after itself. The plants in the following section are a guide only and may not be suitable for every garden, depending on your aspect, exposure and soil type. For assurance on choices check with your local professional gardener.

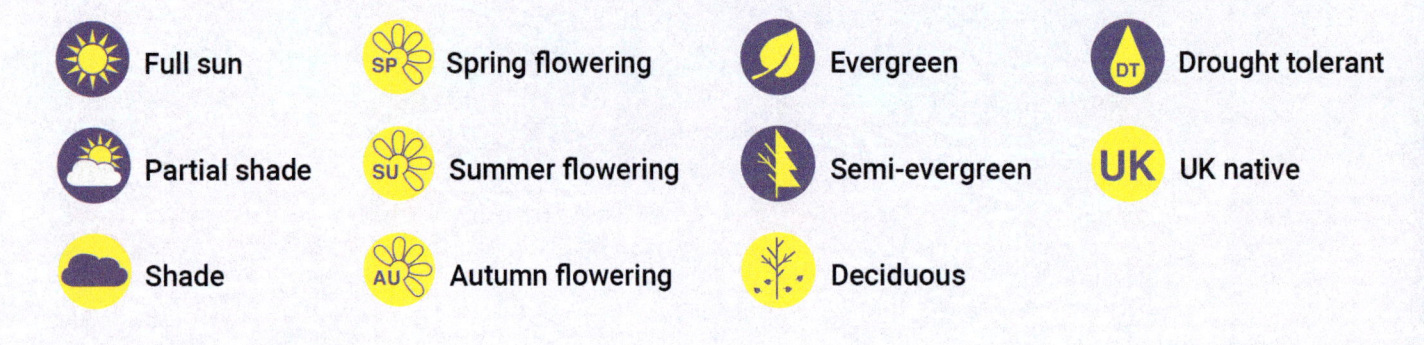

☀ Full sun	SP Spring flowering	🍃 Evergreen	DT Drought tolerant
⛅ Partial shade	SU Summer flowering	🌲 Semi-evergreen	UK UK native
☁ Shade	AU Autumn flowering	🌳 Deciduous	

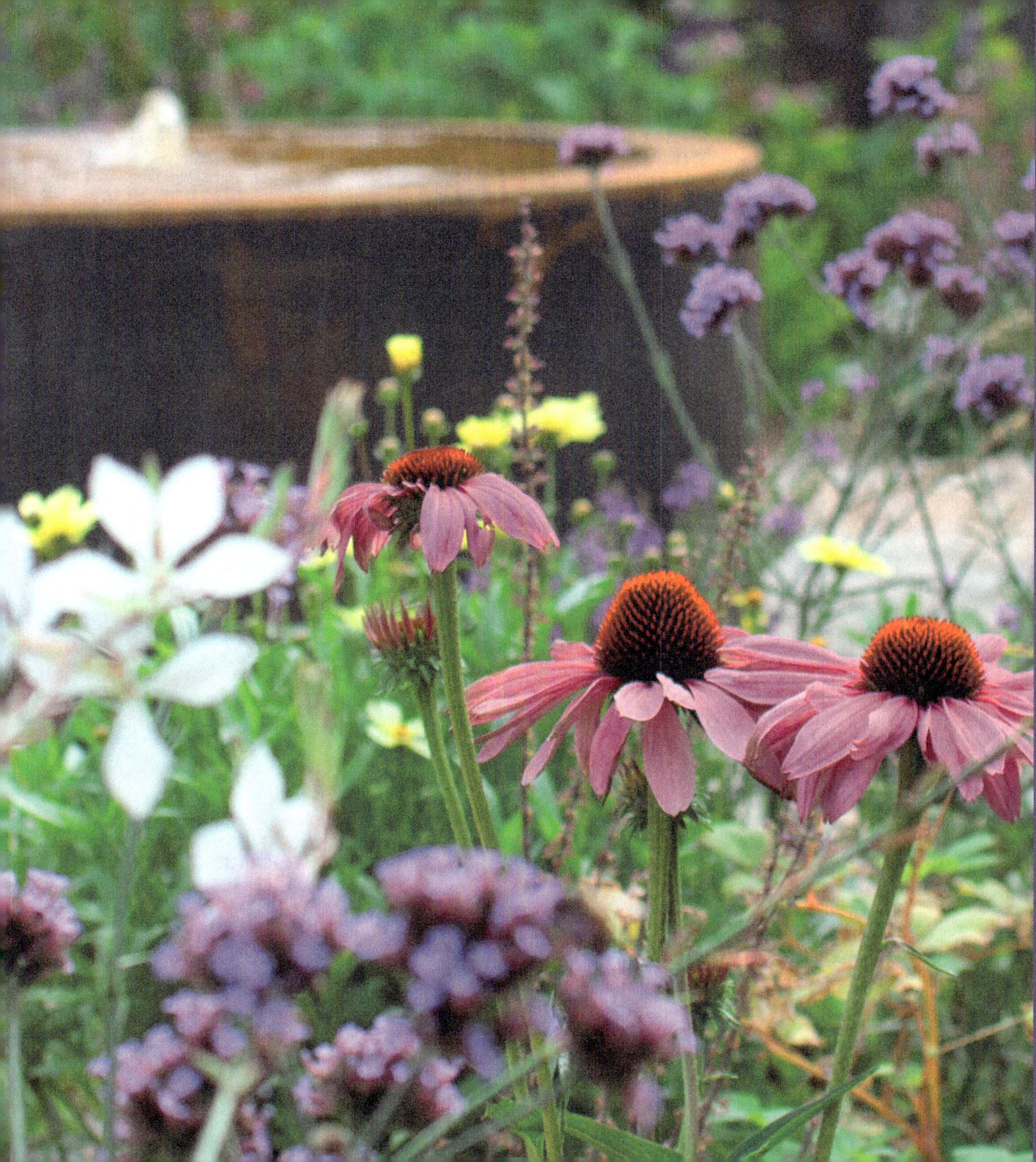

PERENNIALS

Centranthus ruber

A perennial commonly known as valerian, it has grey-green leaves and dense clusters of crimson flowers. Abundant in coastal locations, it spreads efficiently. Spread 0.6m - Height 0.9m

Dipsacus fullonum

A biennial, with spiky blue flowerheads, great for attracting insects. The seedheads give a structural look and can be very popular with goldfinches. Spread 0.3m - Height 1.8m

Lotus corniculatus

A bright perennial whose yellow flowers emerge from the mid-green foliage that sprawls across the ground. This low perennial looks fantastic in a flower bed or amongst shingle. Spread 0.5m - Height 0.3m

Echium vulgare

A bristly biennial that flowers later in the summer. *Echium* grows wild very successfully in coastal areas. The flowers are blue to purple and it can get quite bushy. Spread 0.45m - Height 1.2m

Malva sylvestris

The common mallow is a fairly tall, flowering perennial which flowers from the summer through to early autumn. It can fill a large gap in a flower bed very nicely. Spread 1m - Height 1.5m

Achillea 'Moonshine'

Achillea's common name is yarrow and it comes in many different shades from yellows and bronzes to whites and pinks. The wonderful umbrella-like flowers bloom from late spring. Spread 0.5m - Height 0.6m

Kniphofia uvaria

The red hot poker provides a unique and striking addition to the flowerbed and can work well with many other plants. It flowers on long stems during summer months.
Spread 0.6m - Height 1.2m

Agapanthus 'Blue Giant'

A good structural plant, the *Agapanthus* has large purple flowers which sit atop long, green, erect stems. Happy in a flowerbed or in pots, it's easy to maintain. Spread 0.5m - Height 0.6m

Erigeron karvinskianus

A daisy-like perennial that is very good for ground coverage and for encouraging wildlife. It loves a coastal setting and can often be spotted growing happily in cracks of walls. Spread 1m - Height 0.3m

Crambe cordifolia

A fantastic perennial that is underused in our opinion. It's great value for money, delivering a spectacular summer display and very popular with insects. Spreads 1.5m - Height 2.5m

Thymus serpyllum

A spreading variety of thyme, this scented low-growing perennial looks great in shingle and between paving. It will tolerate being trodden on and can easily be kept under control. Spread 0.5m - Height 0.2m

Lychnis coronaria

The rose campion can be grown as a perennial or biennial and provides a vibrant display of magenta flowers floating above silvery leaves. Flowers into late summer and early autumn. Spread 0.5m - Height 0.70m

Veronicastrum fascination

This perennial will give you architectural height in the flowerbed with long, flowering stems that grow to a height of 1m. Produces a stunning display. Spread 1m - Height 1.5m

Hemerocallis

The daylily flowers in summer and is clump-forming allowing for division in the winter months. Available in lots of colours, the leaf texture makes this a favourite in a coastal scheme. Spread 0.6m - Height 0.9m

Eryngium planum

A favourite perennial, popular in various settings, but particularly striking in a coastal scheme. Its blue thistle-like flowerheads stand out in the flowerbed. Spread 0.5m - Height 1m

Stachys byzantina

A low-growing spreader, *Stachys* has silver, furry leaves, and pink flowers during the summer months. It has a tendency to spread quickly, but can be cut back as desired. Spread 1m - Height 0.5m

Phlomis tuberosa

A clump-forming perennial with lovely pink flowers which bloom throughout the spring and summer months and provide columns of seedheads later in the year. Spread 0.5m - Height 1m

Agastache 'blue fortune'

A full perennial with soft blue/purple flowers, it's fantastic for wildlife and looks stunning for much of the summer months. It can get quite bushy and needs space. Spread 0.5m Height 1m

Verbascum adzharicum

This Verbascum gives a striking display of yellow spires. Great for adding structure to a plant scheme and delivering a pop of colour during the summer months. Spread 0.5m - Height 2m

Salvia nemorosa 'Caradonna'

An early flowering Salvia which offers colour throughout spring and into early summer. Drought-tolerant and no need for nutrients, it is ideal for a coastal garden. Spread 0.5m - Height 0.5m

Sedum album

White stonecrop is a fleshy-leaved perennial that almost looks like a mat. It is low-growing and looks good all year as it is evergreen and has lovely flowerheads in summer. Spread 0.5m - Height 0.1m

185

Galium verum

With long stems of yellow flowers in late summer, this is a rather wild-looking plant which works well in drifts within a relaxed and natural style garden. Spread 1.5m - Height 0.5m

Leucanthemum 'White Knight'

Large daisy-like flowers bring a lovely bold and cheery statement to a garden. When deadheaded regularly, it will happily flower throughout the summer months. Spread 0.3m - Height 0.5m

Iris 'dusky challenger'

A dramatic and bold perennial with shimmery, dark purple flowers which can make quite a statement. Clump-forming, it can be easily divided to provide extra plants. Spread 0.6m - Height 1.2m

Allium stipitatum

The Allium bulb is a favourite in many gardens, The heads can be left after flowering and look good with the structural stems. Spread 0.5m - Height 1m

Dierama pulcherrimum

Firework-like flowering spikes spring from this perennial. It looks very elegant swaying in the coastal breeze. It offers height and lovely pink/mauve flowers. Spread 0.5m - Height 1.5m

Eschscholzia californica

These poppies produce an abundance of flowers and are a great coastal plant. To get the most from the flowering, regular deadheading is essential. Spread 0.5m - Height 0.5m

Trachelospermum jasminoides

An evergreen climber with a structured appearance, it is ideal for covering fences. Commonly known as star jasmine, the scent from the white star-like flowers is heavenly.. It will need training as it grows.
Spread 8m - Height 12m

Artemisia 'Powis Castle'

The silver leaf of this wonderful plant provides a dramatic addition to the flower bed. Often grown for the foliage, this bushy plant does have yellow flowers in late summer. Spread 1m - Height 0.5m

Verbena Bonariensis

A real favourite which loves the sun and flowers deep into autumn. Tall stems hold a cluster of small purple flowers and very little foliage. May need supporting in exposed locations. Spread 0.5m - Height 2m

Echinops bannaticus

A dynamic plant with wonderful blue sphere-shaped spiky heads on tall, grey-green stems. It gives great structure in winter and is a very good fit for a coastal scheme. Spread 1m - Height 1.5m

Echinacea purpurea

A tough, bold perennial that is easy to grow and tolerant of dry soil. This plant comes in many different varieties and colours. It also has many supposed healing properties. Spread 0.5m - Height 0.5m

Liatris spicata 'Floristan Violet'

Liatris is a tall perennial with fluffy, bottle-brush flowerheads and spiny leaves on spikes. This particular variety has a beautiful blue-violet flower.
Spread 0.5m - Height 1m

Helleborus foetidus

A wonderful evergreen perennial, its delicate green bell-like flowers are a winter treat and with its lush leaves, will keep looking good throughout the year. Spread 0.5m - Height 1m

Crambe maritima

Probably the most recognisable coastal plant, sea kale looks fantastic in shingle. It has white flowers in spring and is good for winter structure too. Spread 0.5m - Height 1m

Armeria maritima

A dwarf evergreen perennial, great for growing in shingle and covered in pink to red flowers. If you are planting in the flowerbed, keep these to the front. Spread 0.5m - Height 0.3m

Daucus carota

The wild carrot has umbels of white flowers, each with a single deep red nectar-rich floret in the centre. Fantastic for insects or naturalising. Spread 0.5m - Height 0.70m

Silene uniflora

Sea campion is often found growing wild on the beach and is a lovely flowering perennial. If you keep deadheading, this will flower long into summer. Spread 0.5m - Height 0.5m

Salvia amistad

This wonderful perennial has a long flowering period and can last well into December. Bright purple flowers on long stems. It can get quite bushy, so allow space. Spread 1m - Height 1m

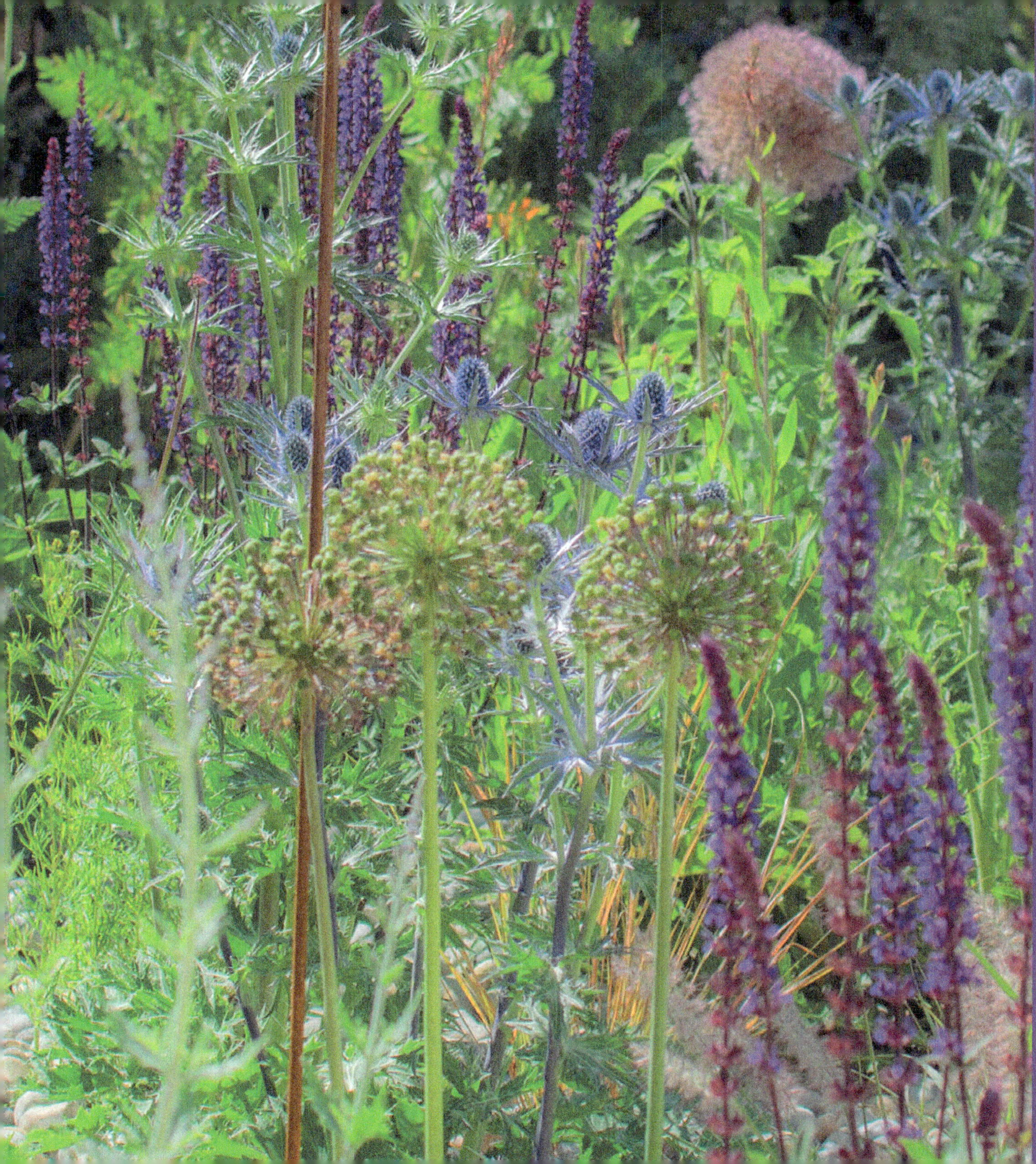

Anemanthele lessoniana (Pheasant's tail grass)

Eryngium bourgatii (Sea holly)

This coastal planting scheme is all about texture! This irregularly spaced layout is reminiscent of the sporadic natural planting along the coast. Wood effect porcelain planks and golden gravel enhances the coastal effect and neutral tones.

Crambe maritima (Sea kale)

Thymus serpyllum (Creeping thyme)

GRASSES

Molinia caerulea

This is a very structural grass and a group planted together can have a very dramatic impact. It looks stunning in autumn with its rich golden colour. Spread 0.5m - Height 1.2m

Stipa tenuissima

If you want something that adds movement and has a soft appearance, look no further. Very wispy and complements shingle and other flowering perennials. Spread 0.3m - Height 0.70m

Phormium tenax

For a jungle or Mediterranean effect the phormium delivers a very strong look. Spiky, this plant can grow rather large and it is worth considering this when planting. Spread 1m - Height 1.5m

Astelia chathamica

A spiky grass with striking silver foliage, it brings great character and can be dotted amongst shingle beds. It can be slightly tender and will need protection during harsh winters. Spread 1m - Height 1.5m

Calamagrostis x acutiflora 'Karl Foerster'

An upright grass with feathery flowering stems, this flows elegantly in the breeze. Works well individually or in great swathes. Spread 1m - Height 1.5m

Panicum virgatum 'Warrior'

This soft, flowing grass looks great in a coastal garden, giving a dramatic effect. Delicate flowers during summer and a turn in colour throughout the seasons. Spread 1m - Height 1m

Hakonechloa macra

A long-lived, tough ornamental grass with eye-catching foliage, the Japanese forest grass can look striking dotted amongst shingle beds. Protect during a harsh winter. Spread 1m - Height 1.5m

Carex

A low-maintenance grass available in various colours, it looks great in shingle beds. It can be slightly tender and will need looking out for during harsh winters. Spread 1m - Height 1.5m

Pennisetum alopecuroides 'Hameln'

A soft grass that flows in the wind and adds delightful texture. In late summer, firework-like flowers appear, which can be left for winter interest. Spread 1m - Height 1m

An avenue of complimentry perennial planting. Coastal gardens can have a rustic look and still be close to the sea. Using old brick paths to compliment buildings helps achieve a balance.

Salvia nemorosa

Hydrangea arborescens 'Annabelle'

Veronicastrum virginicum 'Fascination'

Oenothera lindheimeri

Erigeron karvinskianus

SHRUBS

Pittosporum tenuifolium 'Variegatum'

A tall evergreen with variegated leaves, it works well as natural screening or a windbreak. It does flower, but is usually chosen because it's a practical, bushy shrub. Spread 2m - Height 4m +

Cytisus x kewensis

Commonly known as broom, this is a very low-growing, prostrate shrub. Branches arch with an abundance of cream to yellow flowers in spring. There are many other varieties. Spread 1m - Height 0.30m

Cistus x argenteus 'Silver Ghost'

A low-growing shrub with lovely white, soft cream and pink flowers with yellow centres. It is a bushy, evergreen shrub, so very handy for winter interest. Spread 0.5m - Height 0.70m

Lavandula x intermedia 'Edelweiss'

Lavender brings purple to mind, but this variety is a little different. The edelweiss has white flowers, but is just as lovely and just as fragrant as the traditional plant. Spread 0.5m - Height 0.5m

Pittosporum tobira 'Nanum'

Low-growing, low maintenance and evergreen, this is a popular choice offering good structure in the winter months. The shape is rounded and quite formal. Spread 1m - Height 1m

Ceanothus 'Blue Mound'

Evergreen and bushy with lovely blue flowers, this is a popular shrub that stands out. Pretty blue flowers erupt in late spring and really add depth. It can grow large. Spread 2.5m - Height 1.5m

Mahonia japonica

Mahonia is a spiky evergreen shrub which can be very useful for area coverage. Bright yellow flowers cover the shrub from winter to early spring. Spread 2m - Height 1.5m

Tamarix tetrandra

A real coastal loving shrub, it can grow very large and has arching stems and an abundance of pink or white feathery flowers in the spring. Spread 4m - Height 4m

Santolina chamaecyparissus

A dwarf evergreen shrub with a feathery appearance. *Santolina* can spread across a large area. Silvery leaves bounce nicely with yellow flowerheads. Spread 1m - Height 0.5m

Teucrium fruticans

An evergreen with white, hairy stems and small dark green and white leaves. In the summer these stems produce light blue flowers Likes a sheltered spot. Spread 1.5m - Height 1.5m

Pinus mugo

A large evergreen with short, dark green needles and dark brown, ovoid cones. In spring it produces golden flowers. Suitable for gravel gardens. Little maintenance required. Spread 1m - Height 0.5m

Cordyline australis

Vigorous in growth with a classic palm look, it provides a statement. Long, spiky leaves and spikes of tiny flowers appearing in summer. These can be pruned each year. Spread 1m - Height 4m

Salvia 'blue spire'

If you have an area that needs filling with good structure, this is a nice option. It will bulk and bush out. Blue flowers appear in spring on long stems. Spread 1m - Height 1m

Euphorbia characias subsp. wulfenii

A large evergreen perennial with bright green flower heads and large leaves. Its vertical and arching stems grow from a crown type base. Spread 1m - Height 1m

Rosa rugosa

Tough and disease resistant, these roses are happy almost anywhere. Vigorous, dense growth and beautiful pink flowers make this a lovely hedging option. Spread 2.4m - Height 2.4m

Escallonia rubra

An evergreen shrub which is often used for hedging. This variety has lovely pink/red flowers in summer. It can get large and is good for windbreak or for additional privacy. Spread 3m - Height 4m+

Elaeagnus pungens

A large, solid and hardy evergreen shrub, this is fantastic used as a windbreak. They can grow quickly and will need pruning to keep to the desired height. Spread 4m - Height 4m

Hebe 'Sapphire'

There are many different varieties of Hebe with a huge range of colours and sizes. Many will suit the coastal garden and they always prove to be very durable and reliable. Spread 1.5m - Height 1.5m

Euonymus fortunei 'silver queen'

A slow growing semi-evergreen shrub, usually chosen for the foliage, this is a great shrub for creating form in beds or a low-growing hedge. Spread 1m - Height 1m

Ulex europaeus

Gorse thrives in the coastal air and is covered in coconut-scented, bright yellow flowers in late winter and spring. This is a thorny shrub that packs a punch. Spread 2.5m - Height 2m

Brachyglottis compacta 'sunshine'

A solid shrub with small silvery-tinged leaves which are enhanced with yellow flowers around early summer. Spread 2m - Height 1.5m

TREES

Hippophae rhamnoides

A small tree, sometimes classified as a shrub. Non descript flowers in spring followed by a mass of orange berries in summer. Spread 4m+ Height 4m+

Sorbus aucuparia 'Pendula'

This is a weeping style tree, this produces berries in red, white, yellow, brown or orange depending on variety. It also has delicate white flowers. Good for Autumn colour. Spread 3m - Height 3m

Carpinus betulus

Hornbeam tree, which can also be used for hedging or pleached trees. It is a large tree which will tolerate the sea air. This is also native to Britain. Spread 5m+ - Height 10m+

200

Crataegus monogyna

The Common Hawthorn can be grown as a hedge or shrub and is found commonly around the coast. Scented flowers adorn the tree in spring followed by dark red fruit in autumn. Spread 8m - Height 8m

Cupressus sempervirens

A beautiful evergreen, upright conifer that is tough and hardy and easy to grow, the Mediterranean cypress is a bold addition and ideal in a formal setting. Spread 4m - Height 12m

Quercus ilex

The Holm oak tree is tolerant of salt-spray and sturdy, so very happy growing in a coastal environment. It is a tall evergreen, so can be a good choice for privacy. Spread 5m+ - Height 10m+

Ginkgo biloba

Very desirable for the attractive leaf, the Ginkgo will grow into a lovely shape and adds interest to a flowerbed. It is happiest in a sheltered position. Spread 3m - Height 5m+

Ilex aquifolium

Holly trees will cope very well with harsh coastal conditions. A durable evergreen with spiky leaves and bright red berries in the winter. Great for privacy or a windbreak. Spread 3m - Height 8m+

Pinus nigra 'maritima'

The Pine is a true coastal tree with a structure that works really well visually. They grow tall and will drop leaves, but it is evergreen and looks good all year. Spread 5m+ - Height 8m+

PLANTING SCHEMES

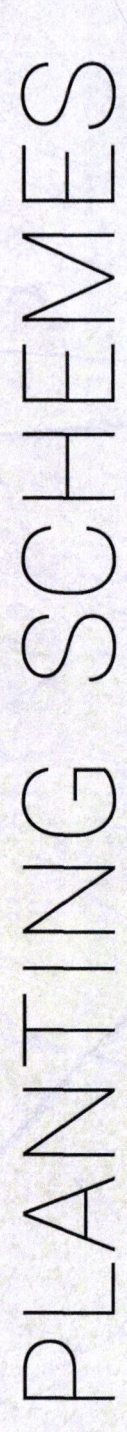

Planning your plant scheme is all about putting together a collection of plants that compliment each other and creating a balanced look throughout your garden. There needs to be balance between textures and fullness and consistently following your colour scheme is vital.

Because plants have differing light and water preferences, prefer different sites and vary a great deal in size, shape and colour, a properly considered planting scheme is essential to get the best end result for your garden. The plant selection on the opposite page gives an indication of a selection of plants that work well together as a group in a bed.

On the following pages there are examples of planting schemes with plant identification names to help. You will also find a guide on how to create a planting plan, which should help you work out where to plant what within your scheme.

Some plants work to give great ground cover, such as *sedum*; some act as bulk that fill large spaces, such as *Euphorbia characias;* and some are more animated, blowing in the wind and cutting through the foliage with popping colours, such as *verbena*. Each has its own role within a garden scheme and this next chapter will help to support your plant choices.

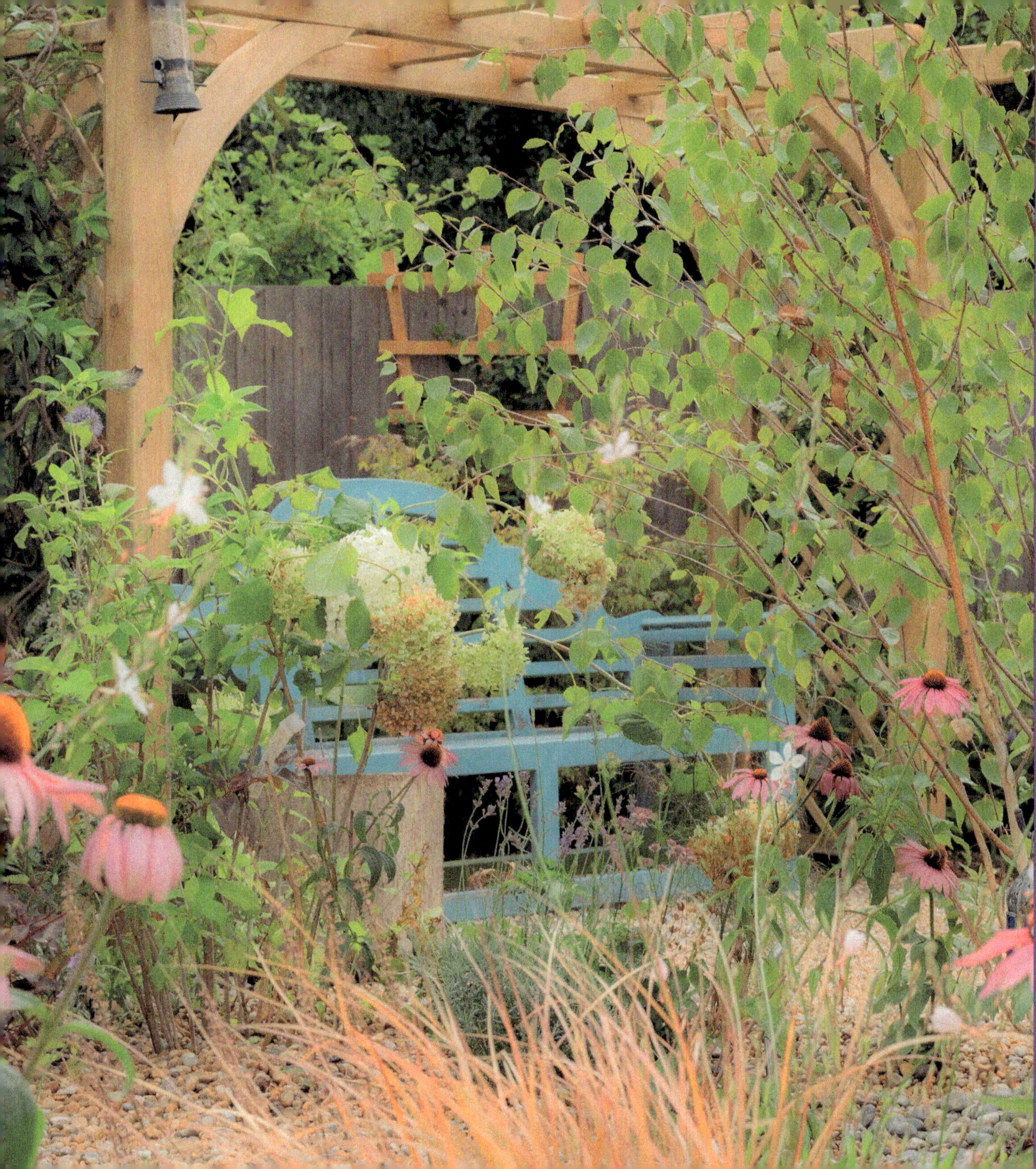

LAYOUT STYLES

IRREGULAR

Irregular planting means spreading out the same plants throughout the bed. This is a common method used in smaller beds and irregular-shaped beds. If you want to create a wild-effect garden this would be a good layout.

FOCAL

A focal point can be a large plant or a feature such as an ornate pot. Place the focal first and place the plants around it. Eventual height is important to consider to ensure the plants do not grow taller than the feature.

LINEAR

Ideal for formal gardens based on clean, straight lines. This layout style is relatively easy to complete by using low-growing plants in the front rows and larger plants at the back. This approach can be very effective when planting in rows according to colour.

CLUSTER

This layout creates a stunning swathe effect, especially when you use grasses. It's recommended you plant them in groups of odd numbers like 3s, 5s and 7s. Large clusters of plants in large planting beds can be very effective.

EXAMPLE LAYOUT

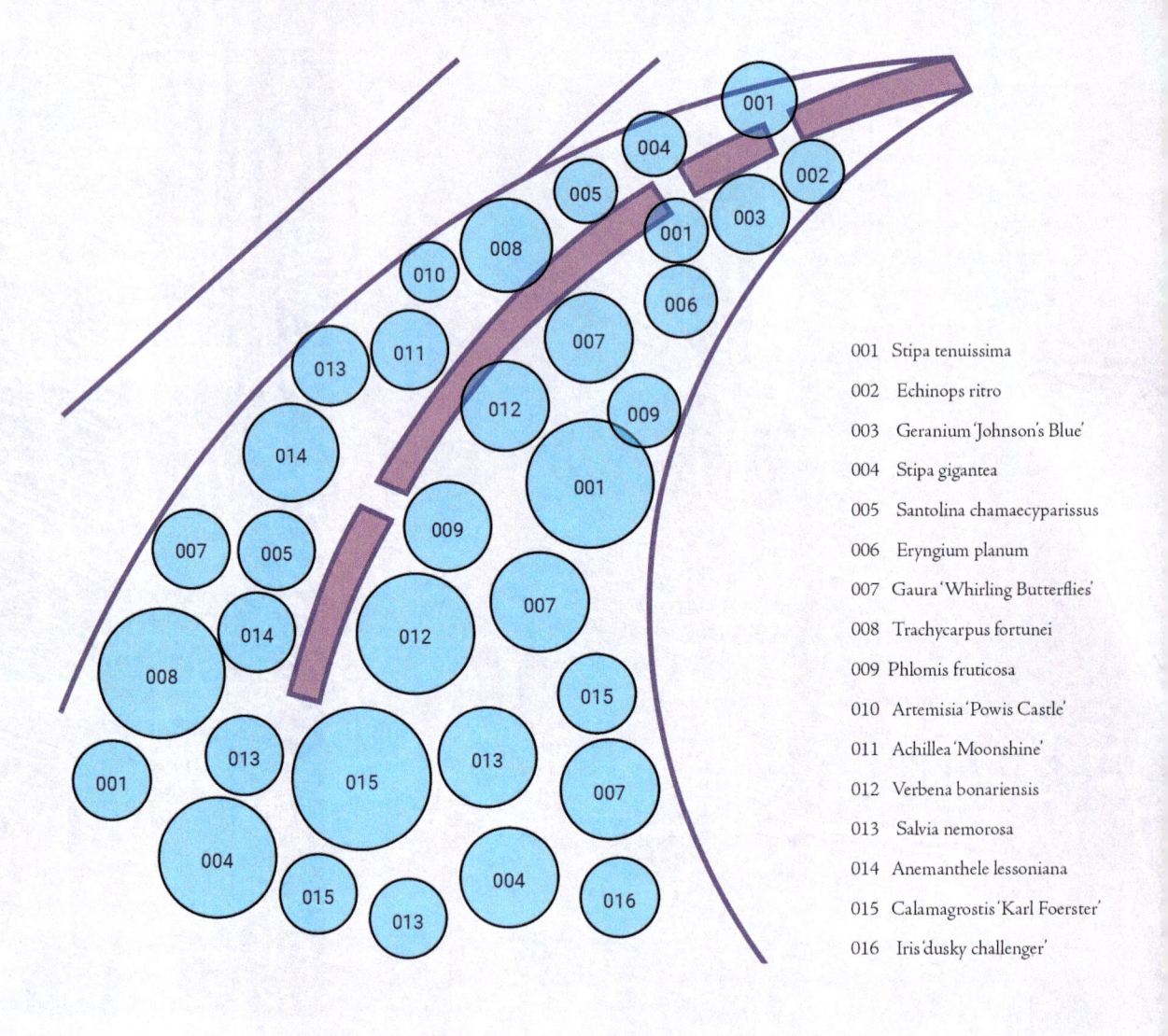

001	Stipa tenuissima
002	Echinops ritro
003	Geranium 'Johnson's Blue'
004	Stipa gigantea
005	Santolina chamaecyparissus
006	Eryngium planum
007	Gaura 'Whirling Butterflies'
008	Trachycarpus fortunei
009	Phlomis fruticosa
010	Artemisia 'Powis Castle'
011	Achillea 'Moonshine'
012	Verbena bonariensis
013	Salvia nemorosa
014	Anemanthele lessoniana
015	Calamagrostis 'Karl Foerster'
016	Iris 'dusky challenger'

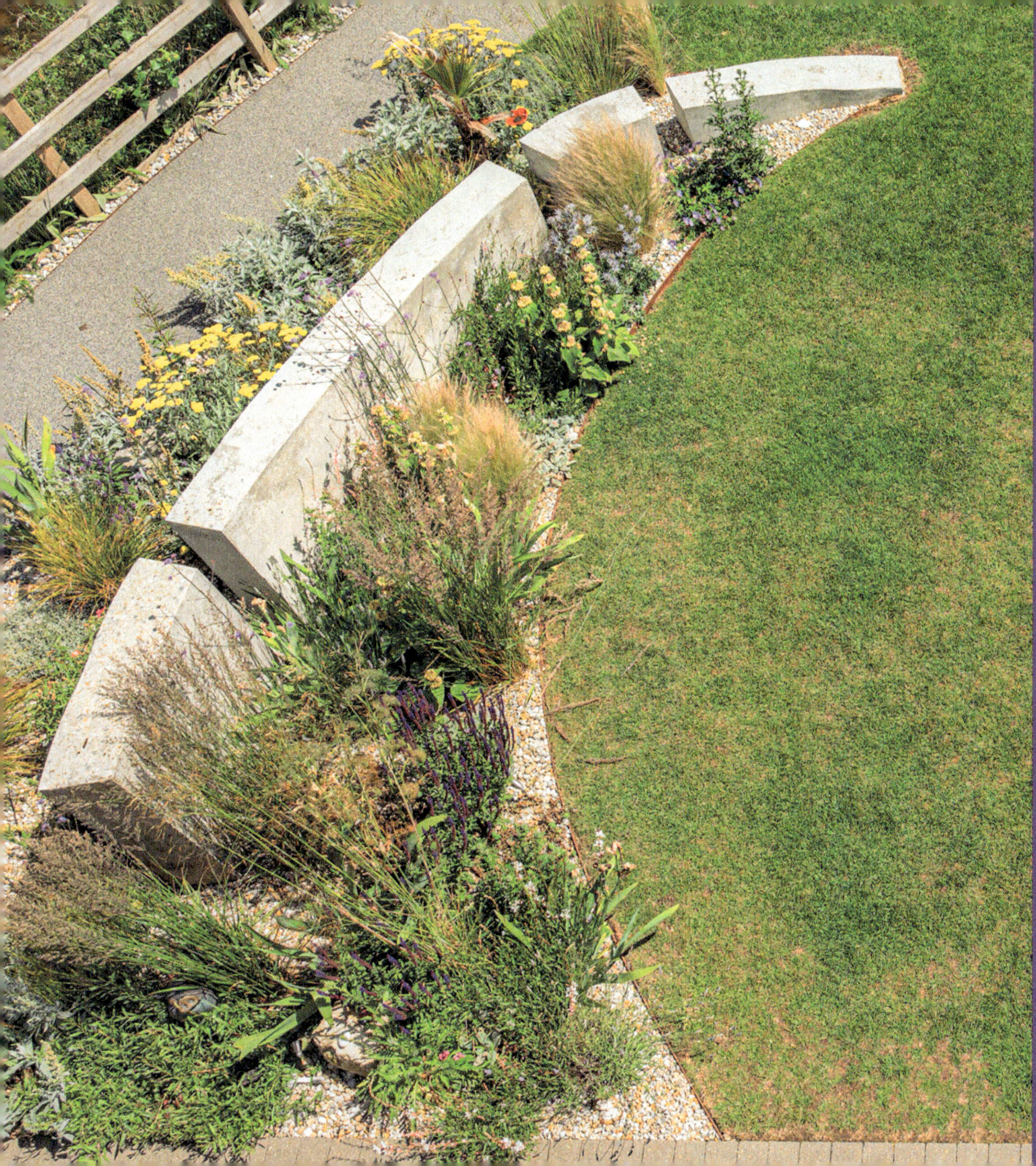

DRAWING PLANTING

01

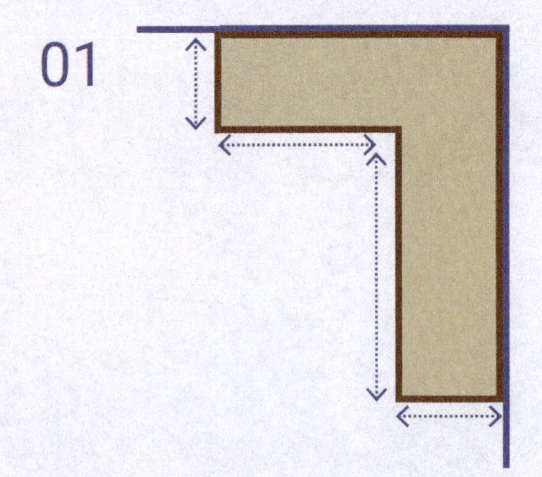

Use the detailed sketch of your garden design to get the measurements of the planting bed. This is important to ensure that you get the balance right between having a beautiful, full bed and an overcrowded area. This example is based on an irregular style with a focal point.

02

Create a mood board of plants. Choose the plants you like from the plant guide, considering the balance of textures and colours. Think about whether your bed is in full sun, partial sun or shade and which plants will suit the type of soil it contains. Don't forget to consider how the plants will look throughout the seasons.

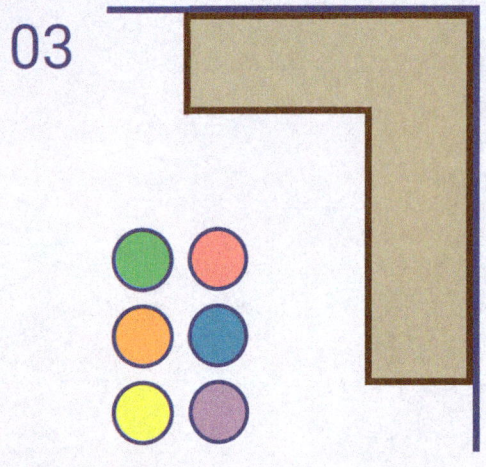

03

Draw the outline of your plant bed to scale. Begin by drawing the largest plants in the scheme. Use colour coding to differentiate between the plants. It is always best to plant in odd numbers of each species.

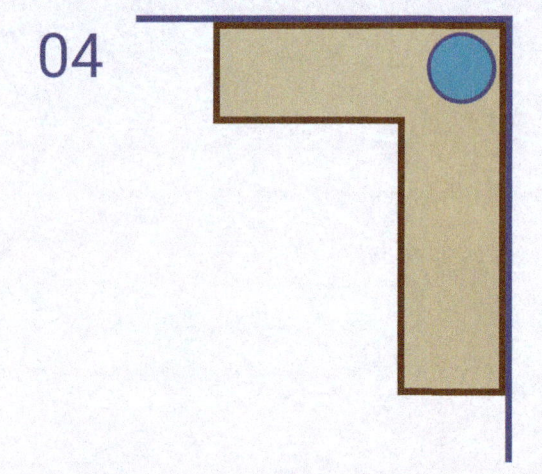

04

Using a scaled circular ruler, draw a circle that represents the size that the largest focal species will grow to. Large plants are best placed in the centre of the bed or towards the back depending on the location and shape.

05

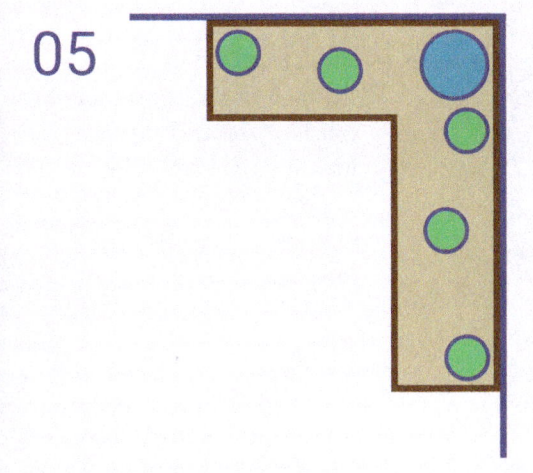

If you have chosen any evergreen shrubs, draw these in the border next, remembering to base the space on the eventual size. Spread them to create a general structure.

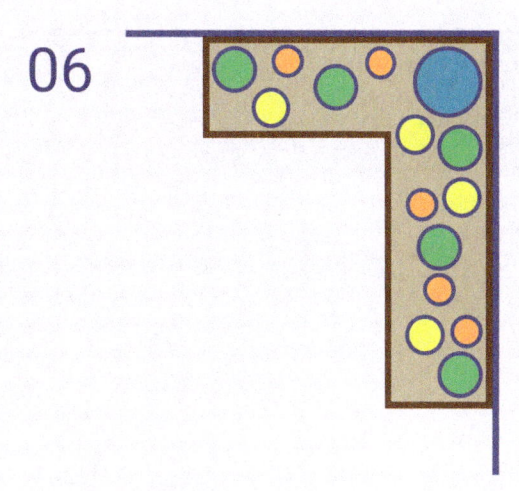

06

Start drawing in any ornamental grasses next and then any larger perennials. These are best spaced and planted throughout the bed.

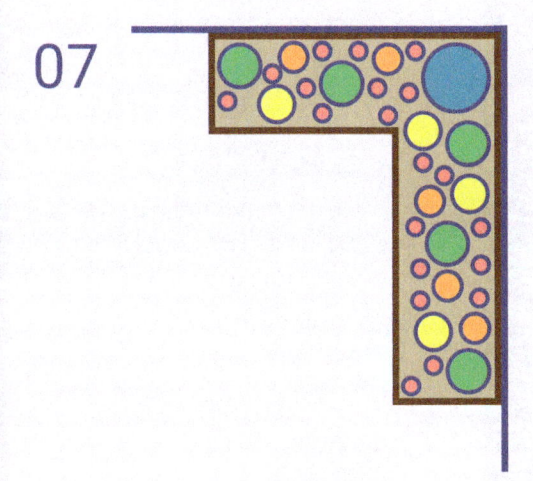

07

Next, draw in the smaller perennials, spreading them throughout the bed. These can be placed individually or in groups for a stronger impact.

08

Lastly, the lower ground plants need to be placed at the front of the bed. Now you have your design, you can be confident that, provided the plants stay happy, you will have your perfect bed.

PLANTING LAYOUT

HEIGHT
This is a *Dicksonia Antarctica* tree fern. As you can see its trunk rises above the underplanting and has fronds creating an upper level of interest.

SEASONAL
This display is jungle themed which means that most of the plants are evergreen.

TEXTURE
This *Fatsia japonica* has large and attractive textural leaves.

SPACING
This layout is full but well balanced. The space given has been successfully considered to ensure maximum coverage.

COLOUR
Heuchera is a good example of how considering leaf colour can add impact and balance a scheme well.

HEIGHT

The image opposite represents a typical border. The finished height of the plants in your scheme is an important factor. The standard theory is to plant lower at the front and work backwards, adding increasingly taller plants as you go, ending with tallest plants at the rear, but in many circumstances it can be useful to add some lower planting in between to add depth to the bed. If a plant is particularly structural, you can dot lower planting around it to help draw the eye.

Finally, if you have an island bed, why not consider mounding plants in the centre. This gives you the opportunity to use lower planting around it with the height already in place.

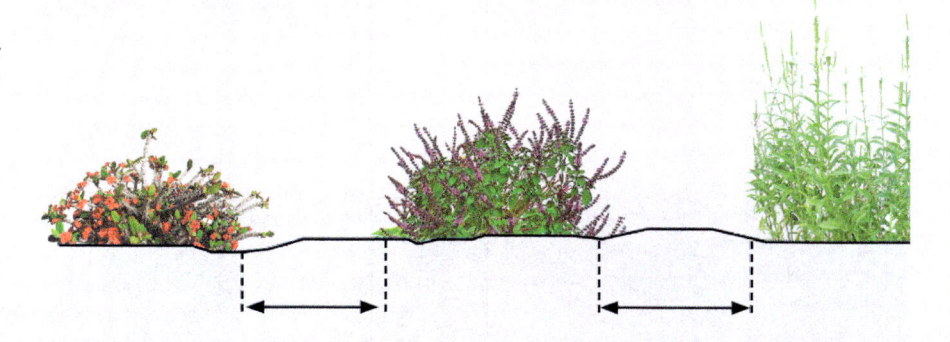

SPACING

Plant spacing is an important factor. It is vital to allow the correct distance between plants to allow for their 3 year growth. Whilst this may look rather sparse initially, given time it will fill in. If you desire more of an instant show, you could infill gaps with annuals.

If you want a dotted beach look in shingle, you may not want fully grown plants to touch each other. Allowing space between the plants will give them all plenty of room to stretch their roots out underground over time.

SEASONAL INTEREST

Seasonal interest is easily achieved with a coastal design. Shrubs provide a good basic structure to a bed and are very often evergreen. Grasses and taller perennials can follow - think about flowering times and when they need to be pruned back.

It is nice to have something to look forward to throughout the seasons and careful consideration of flowering times will help you achieve this.

During the winter months, grasses still look good and structural plants will look stunning with their seedheads on display.

Evergreen Shrubs

211

PROLONGED COLOUR

Here is a great example of a well-thought-out bed which has developed over a number of years. A relatively modest selection of plants has been used, but they all flower for a good period of time.

You can see how the planting and colours have weaved and blended together to create a lovely natural look. The varied textures add interest and show them all off. This is a coastal bed less than 100 metres from the sea, so it is a good indication of just how well plants can thrive in this habitat.

SALVIA NEMOROSA

ACHILLEA 'MOONSHINE'

STACHYS BYZANTINA 'SILVER CARPET'

ERYNGIUM BOURGATII

SUMMER FLOWERING

Clustered and linear plant layouts work really well for a summer flowering bed, ensuring a really good show throughout those key months.

The colour palette can be anything you like - there are so many options with summer flowers.

It can be very effective to use large groups of same-species plants in repeated clusters throughout the scheme.

AGAPANTHUS INAPERTUS

RUDBECKIA FULGIDA

HYDRANGEA ARBORESCENS 'ANNABELLE'

SEDUM TELEPHIUM

212

MEDITERRANEAN

Having some statement trees in amongst low-level clusters of plants is a great way to replicate a Mediterranean bed. A lot of silvers and greens with some large clusters of colour creates a beautiful effect leading the eye through the bed.

If you add large focal points or features such as boulders, consider how it will look long-term. Will the plants around them eventually spread or swamp your feature?

ERIGERON KARVINSKIANUS

TEUCRIUM FRUTICANS

LAVANDULA AUGUSTIFOLIA 'MUNSTED'

CISTUS CRETICUS

VIBRANT

Vibrant beds are very often designed using an irregular layout style, giving areas of bright colour with little order. Depending on the size of your bed, you can bring in large clusters of colour which can be striking.

If you want to enhance vibrancy, consider the colours of each plant and pair them near plants with complementary or contrasting colour to really make the bed come to life.

GAURA 'WHIRLING BUUTERFLIES'

ACHILLEA 'MOONSHINE'

ARMERIA

SALVIA NEMOROSA

ENVIRONMENTAL CONSIDERATIONS

12

Research has shown time and again that gardens are extremely valuable habitats, essential for supporting wildlife and biodiversity. A garden designed and managed with wildlife in mind brings a whole new dimension of interest to a beautiful space. Supporting biodiversity allows a garden to develop naturally, which, as a result, becomes much easier to manage.

A coastal garden may have elements that are not necessarily associated with wildlife, but just because your garden might have focal points which include gravel, drought-tolerant plants and metal sculptures, it certainly doesn't mean that it can't be wildlife-friendly.

A biodiverse garden can be created by considering how every element will affect its inhabitants or would-be inhabitants. If you want visitors, how does a garden element offer food and shelter?

Plants that attract insects are a great place to start. Insects attract birds, reptiles, mammals - any creature inclined to think of them as food.

Many of the plants suggested in this book are very good options for attracting pollinators during the warmer months and some keep their seed heads throughout winter too.

Ladybirds and other overwintering insects use empty seed heads to keep safe, warm and protected from the elements. Little nooks and crannies here and there can be prime real estate for many little creatures.

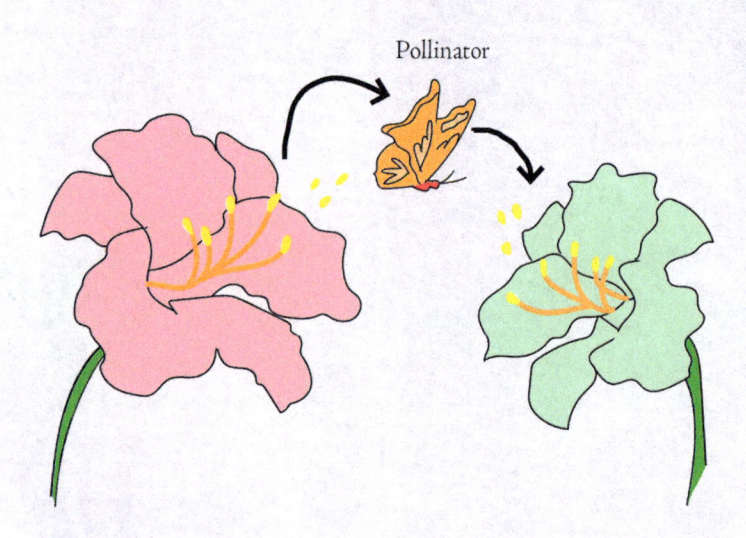

Pollinator

Pollination is crucial to our own survival as a species and depends on many types of insects - it's not just the bees that keep things going- beetles, moths, butterflies, hoverflies and other flies are also essential pollinators in the UK.

A key element to developing a natural space buzzing with wildlife is water. This is obviously a major part of coastal areas as well, so sits very nicely within a coastal garden design. Water is essential to life - a new pond or water feature quickly develops from an unremarkable body of water into an incredible little microcosm.

Consigning your feature to the edge of your garden may seem like a good idea to avoid disturbing visiting wildlife, but it reduces the available planting area around the edge and may not be so easily enjoyed by you.

If you can surround the water with vegetation, timid creatures are more likely to investigate because of the extra protection.

A water butt is a great addition to any garden, coastal or not. Collecting rain water is a great way to make sure you are able to give all your plants extra water when needed – and rain water is best of all.

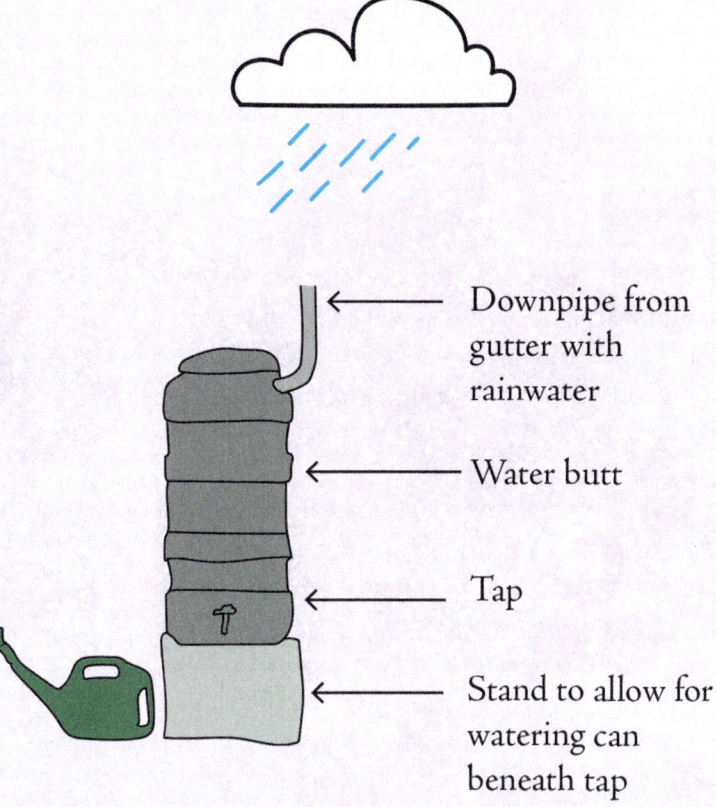

Life attracts life and the life gets bigger and more noticeable. Before long, your whole garden is teeming with it.

And so it goes on. One day you'll hopefully be treated to the thrilling glimpse of a hedgehog snuffling in the undergrowth looking for a good place to lean in and get a much needed drink or a little frog popping its head through the water surface.

When designing your pond or water feature, consider how wildlife will get in and out of the water safely and how you will access it when needed.

← Downpipe from gutter with rainwater

← Water butt

← Tap

← Stand to allow for watering can beneath tap

Compost heaps are another wildlife magnet to include in a garden design. Not only do they offer shelter and food for insects, reptiles and other wildlife, but they are the answer to your prayers when trying to get rid of garden waste. From earwigs and slugs to slow worms and frogs, a compost heap is a wonderful place for a creature to hide, feed and reproduce.

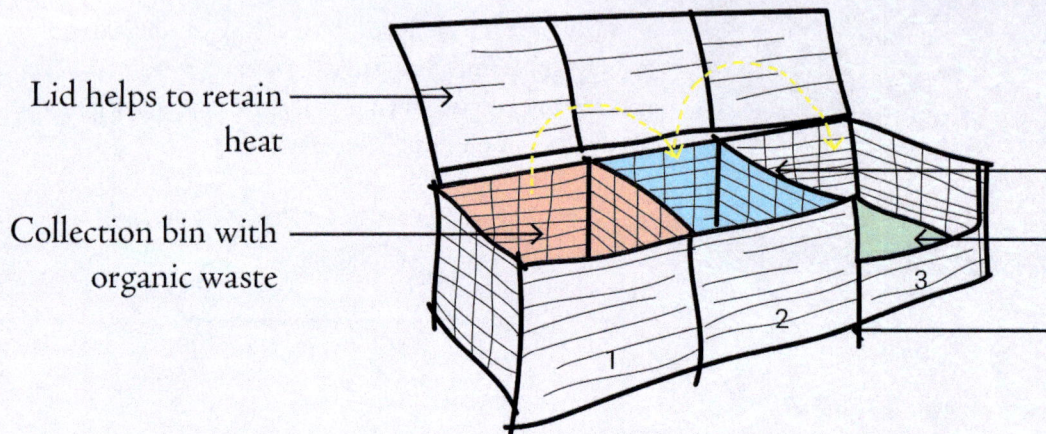

Lid helps to retain heat

Collection bin with organic waste

Overtime, waste from bin 1 shrinks and is moved to bin 2

Finished compost to use in the garden

Removable front panels

Considering how you can encourage wildlife into your coastal garden will ensure that you're rewarded with a vibrant garden full of life and the satisfaction of knowing you've made a difference.

Wild garden visitors do not care how beautiful your space is and if you can leave a corner of a grassy area alone for a couple of months, many of them will be very grateful. Leaving grass long improves conditions for invertebrates, offering them shelter and places to grow and hatch in peace. Of course, more invertebrates means more mammals and birds, which is a bonus for all.

Of course, it goes without saying that sourcing natural and sustainable elements for your coastal garden is preferable to buying new. Considering how you can encourage wildlife into your coastal garden will ensure that you're rewarded with a vibrant garden full of life and the satisfaction of knowing you've made a difference.

ENJOY YOUR

FINISHED GARDEN

IVY & WHYTE
GARDEN DESIGN

KENT AND SUSSEX

Ivy & Whyte comprises of two studios, in Brighton, East Sussex and Hythe, Kent. We absolutely love having our creative practices on the coast and it allows us to take inspiration from our direct surroundings. Discovering exciting and unusual materials, colours and plants allows us to create inspired designs that are dynamic and diverse.

The practice hosts a collaborative balance with our team's knowledge in landscaping, horticulture, art and architecture. At Ivy & Whyte we all began our creative journey through an artistic venture.

Although we are coastal garden design specialists, our projects are all immensely varied, from Kentish country gardens to small tropical gardens, we do it all, and we are passionate about every design we produce. We are always bold, artistic and unique in our approach to design.

Annabelle, Ivy & Whyte Sussex.

Mark, Ivy and Whyte Kent.

WITH THANKS:

We would like to offer our sincere thanks to everyone involved in the book and in paricular the gardens that feature.

John Humphreys - johnhumphreyssculpture.com

Becca Duncan - www.blossominggardens.co.uk

Sue Townsend - www.suetownsendgardendesign.co.uk

Kim Parish - www.landscapesofdistinction.co.uk

Sara Hopgood and Peter Lendray of PS Gardens - page 106

Sharon Head - Normans Bay Sussex - page 106

Robert Barker Garden Design - robertbarkerdesign.com - page143

London Stone - www.londonstone.co.uk

Charmaine Ferguson

Annabelle Hodd

Ian Barrett

Tony and Diane Shepherd

Annabel Squires

Paul and Gill Howes

Celine Lynch

Helen Thompson

Bethany Whyte

Holly Whyte

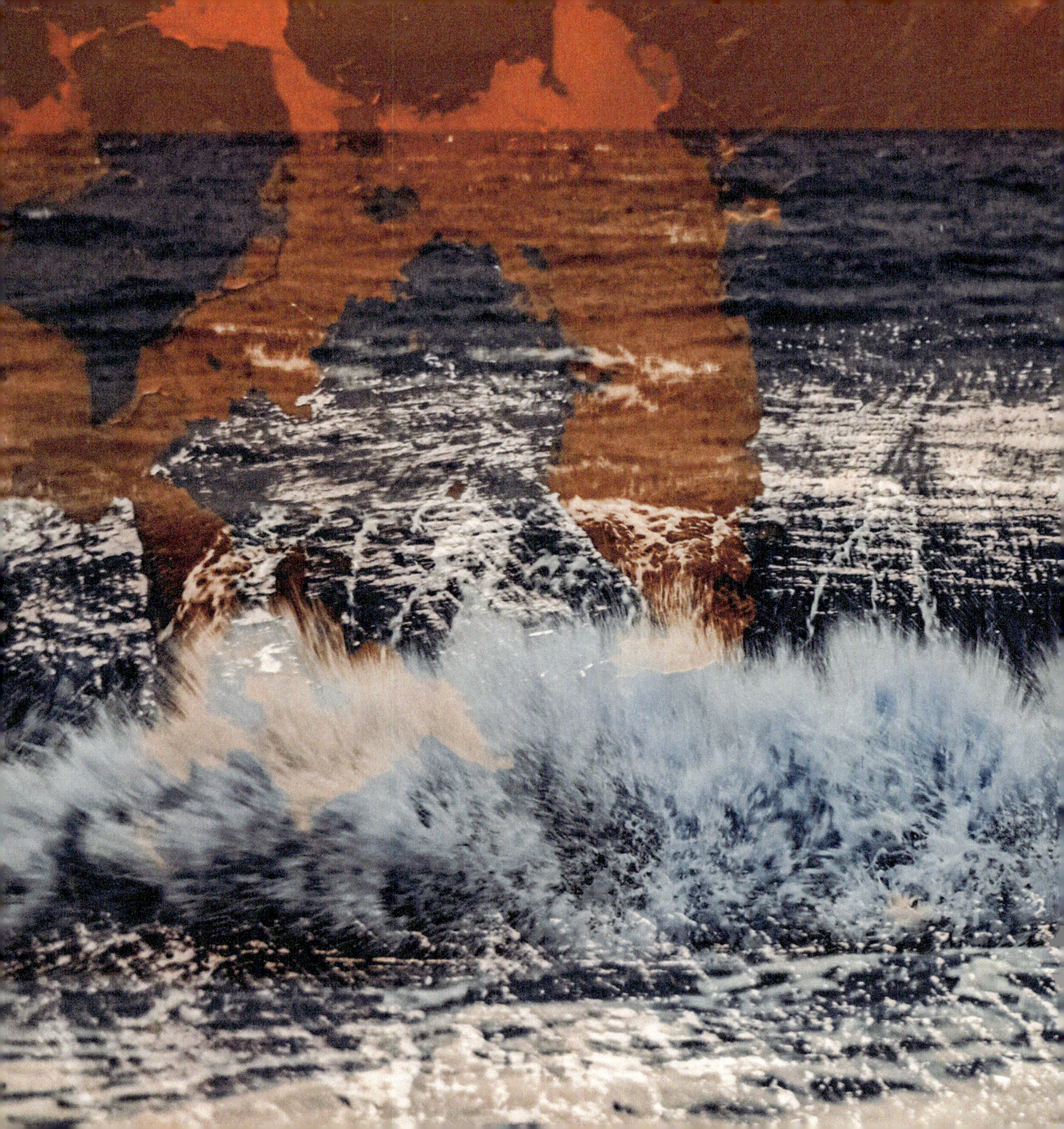

Printed in Great Britain
by Amazon